Make Hay
While *the* Sun Shines

Fourth in the Series
of Stories About Growing Up
in and Around Small Towns in the Midwest

edited by Jean Tennant

Shapato Publishing
Everly, Iowa

Published by: Shapato Publishing, LLC
        PO Box 476
        Everly, IA 51338

ISBN 13: 978-0615534350
ISBN 10: 061553435X

Library of Congress Control Number: 2011918858
Copyright © 2011 Shapato Publishing

First Printing November 2011
Front cover photo provided by Carolyn Rohrbaugh
Back Cover photo provided by Glenn Lynn
Original artwork by LaVonne M. Hansen

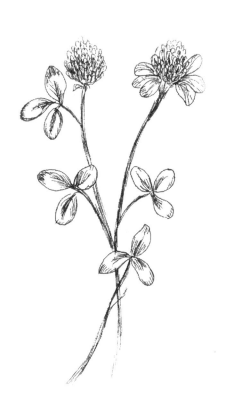

T his book would not be possible without the talented writers who continue to share their stories, as well as their many wonderful pictures, portraying life in the Midwest. Without them, these memories might be lost. With them, our lives are infinitely richer.

I also must take a moment to thank our proofreaders, Anji and Carolyn, who so diligently hunted for those annoying misspellings, dropped or misused words, and typos that seem to haunt any piece of writing. If any errors did slip through—and it's inevitable, something *will*—I take full responsibility.

Jean Tennant
Shapato Publishing, LLC
Everly, Iowa

Photo provided by Grover Reiser

TABLE OF CONTENTS

Make Hay
While *the* Sun Shines

Fourth in the Series
of Stories About Growing Up
in and Around Small Towns in the Midwest

Photo provided by Lyle Ernst

BIRD AND DOLLY
Lyle Ernst

"**M**aking hay" on the farm in the 1940s was not my idea of fun. I would much rather have been sitting on the bank of Brush Creek with my cane pole, catching some trout, or running along the bluffs playing Cowboys and Indians all by myself.

We lived on my Grandpa's farm, nestled in the hills of Jackson County, Iowa. The terrain was rough and hilly, but my dad made the best of it.

Thank goodness for Bird and Dolly, Dad's dapple-gray horses. The three of them were best friends and had been together for a long time. During hay making season Bird and Dolly's job consisted of pulling the hay mower, the hay rake and the hay wagon. Dad took special care of them. They were brushed and curried every night and always had plenty of food and water.

When Dad worked in the field up on the ridge it was my job to take him his lunch. Money was scarce and lunch usually consisted of a couple of fried egg sandwiches, a piece of cake and some of Mom's homemade lemonade. Dad would unhitch Bird and Dolly, and all of us retreated to a big shade tree.

I recall the time when Dad injured his hand while repairing the hay rake. The entire field of hay on the ridge was ready to be put up in the barn, and the weather forecast was rain. Dad knew a man named Billy who lived by himself and worked at odd jobs. Billy's favorite pastime was drinking beer, and once he got started he wouldn't stop until he ran out of money, then he would find odd jobs until his thirst for beer got the best of him.

Dad knew this, but with the weatherman predicting rain he was desperate, so after finding Billy enjoying his "suds" at a local tavern, Dad convinced him to help make hay that day, overlooking the fact that Billy was on one of his drinking binges.

Dad and Billy arrived at the farm and Dad promptly harnessed Bird and Dolly to the hay wagon, hooked the hay loader on behind it, and with me handling the reins and Billy on the wagon, we commenced to make hay.

Things were going smoothly with Bird and Dolly, as always, performing their jobs to perfection. Billy was pitching the hay evenly on the wagon, getting it stacked higher and higher, making it more difficult to see him. After a time, I noticed hay was falling off the wagon. I stopped Bird and Dolly and walked to the side of the wagon in an effort to see what Billy was doing. He was nowhere around, and the hay that should have been stacked neatly on the wagon, was trailing on behind.

Far off in the distance, I could see Billy lying on the ground. I ran to him, scared of what I was going to find. When I reached him I asked, "Billy, are you all right?"

He answered, "I think so."

Billy always wore a hat that resembled the type a captain of a ship might wear, and he always kept his pipe inside it. His hat was still on his head, but the pipe was broken. I managed to help him up; he said he was okay, so we finished the load of hay and returned to the barn with it. Dad and Billy both laughed about Billy's fall and we continued to make hay, although occasionally Billy would complain about his neck hurting.

The next morning when Dad went to get Billy for haying, he found him in great pain and unable to move. Dad took him directly to the nearest hospital where the doctor diagnosed Billy with a broken neck. The doctor said that if Billy had been sober he might have died. He recovered with no after affects, but I don't remember him helping us make hay after that.

When it came time to hoist the hay into the haymow, Dolly and I became important participants. Dad would hitch Dolly to the hayfork to which he would attach a long rope. My job was to walk Dolly as she was pulling the rope, until Dad yelled "Whoa," at which time I would stop Dolly and he would trip the hayfork, thus dropping the hay at the spot in the haymow that he desired. I was a young shaver at that time, and walking Dolly back and forth was a very boring job that seemed to go on forever.

Sometimes my mother would join me, which would relieve some of the boredom.

The only fun part was being barefoot and able to puddle along in the fine, soft dust that felt so good between my toes. But I also remember the itch of hay chaff down my shirt and in my eyes and hair.

The years were catching up to Bird and Dolly. They had worked hard faithfully all their years and were getting old. Dad, regretfully, decided he would have to sell them and put the money toward buying a tractor. I remember the tractor well. It was a used McCormick Deering F20 with steel wheels.

Dad sold Bird and Dolly to a neighbor who lived up the valley a ways, but only after being assured that they would be looked after and treated kindly.

The day we took them to their new home was one I won't forget. As we drove away, after saying our good-byes, both Bird and Dolly whinnied. I could see the pain in Dad's eyes. There was not a word spoken as we drove home. It was the last time I saw Bird and Dolly.

Making hay would never be the same.

Lyle Ernst enjoys writing both non-fiction and fiction. He has been published in regional magazines, and has three non-fiction books, edited by Robert Wolf, in addition to feature stories in the *Cedar Rapids Gazette* and *Moline Dispatch*. Lyle resides in Davenport, Iowa, with his wife, Pat.

Photo provided by Judy Taber

RAKING HAY
Gene Miller

In the summer of 1980 I made a trip to New Providence, New Jersey, which is right outside of New York City. I was there to visit David Feltman, a college friend of mine who had recently graduated from Princeton Theological Seminary. Dave was serving a church in New Providence as an associate pastor. Among his responsibilities was the congregation's youth ministry.

On one of the evenings I was there, the youth group had a meeting. After the meeting was over and we were standing around visiting and socializing, one of the adults asked Dave and me an interesting question: "Why are you two guys so thick through the shoulders?"

Why are you two guys so thick through the shoulders? I had never been asked a question like that before, and as I surveyed the room I did indeed notice that the urban physiques occupying the room with us were built differently. None of them were, indeed, thick through the shoulders.

Dave and I looked at each other for a few moments and then we both mentioned that maybe it had to do with the fact that we were both Iowa farm boys. We then proceeded to try and explain about the chores and work we had performed growing up on an Iowa farm, and how those chores had naturally affected our physical development. But how can you truly explain to a city dweller who has never set foot on a farm about walking beans, pitching manure, and baling hay?

In this modern era, hay baling can be done by a single person running a baler that makes the round bales, and a forklift to put the bales into storage. It's sometimes difficult to remember the old days, when baling hay was incredibly labor intensive. In my generation bales were square, relatively small, and roughly fifty pounds in weight; they were moved primarily by hand, and stored in a haymow or hayloft. Hay, by the way, is grass, clover or alfalfa that's been cut, dried and baled for fodder. In any given summer there are generally three cuttings, or crops, from the same field or stand.

For many of us, bailing was our initial test of manhood. Once you could throw hay bales with the men, you were considered a man yourself.

I particularly remember my rite of passage. It was the summer after my eighth grade in school and the men were planning to bale hay at my Uncle Joe's. They wanted to get the job done as quickly as possible. So, as fast as they could, they planned to mow it, rake it, bale it, and put it in the barn's haymow. I was still too small to throw bales, but I could drive a tractor by then, so they gave me the job of raking the hay into windrows.

For two days I raked hay ahead of the baler. Each of those days I went with my dad to my uncle's farm, crawled onto his Farmall tractor, drove it to the field and raked the hay. At noon I ate dinner with the men. In the country we call the noon meal dinner, and the evening meal supper, as opposed to city folk who use the terms lunch and dinner, respectively.

I thought eating dinner with the adults was grand. I listened to their conversations, ate hearty, sumptuous food and felt like a grown-up. Occasionally they even asked me what I thought about something. It was great!

The next year I graduated to loading bales on the rack behind the baler. At fourteen and fifteen years of age it's amazing how much one's muscles develop in a year. After that I went to the haymow itself, which, because of the heat that's captured in a barn on hot July days in Iowa, is the hardest part of baling. Sometimes we baled in 90-degree temperatures, and who knows how hot it was in the haymow? We never measured it. I'm not sure I would have wanted to know.

We paced ourselves. We drank lots of water. In between loads we'd sit in the barn's large open front door to take in the fresh country air, and visit until the next load came in from the field.

Baling hay for the neighbors was also a way of making a little extra spending money. A neighbor would call, we'd check with Dad to see if he needed us for anything, and if he said "No," off we'd go for an afternoon or two of throwing hay bales for $1.50 to $2.00 an hour. Afterwards we felt temporarily rich.

All of this kept us in incredibly good physical condition. When it came time to get in shape for sports for the coming school year, we already had a leg up. And it gave us nice, thick shoulders. Shoulders that eventually helped us in life to carry much, much more than hay.

Gene Miller was raised on his great-grandfather's farm one mile east of Lone Rock, Iowa. He is the oldest of five boys, and is co-author of *Heart to Heart: the Little Al Story.* www.littlealfoundation.org.

Photo provided by Kent Stephens

MOWING
Kent Stephens

I got up early, real early. I had a lot of chores that needed to get done. The sun was just starting up. Today was going to be BIG.

It was mid July 1960. I was a suburban California kid staying on the family farm just West of Osceola, Iowa, for the summer. I was sleeping on the screened-in back porch. The dogs, Patty and Mike, slept with me. Uncle Clarence made sure I had everything I needed, a .22 cal single-shot rifle and fishing gear, stationed by the back door, at the ready.

If I finished chores earlier than normal, before Clarence got up, I knew he would fix us breakfast, a real farmer's breakfast of hash-browns, bacon and eggs, with toast and jelly. Most of the breakfast fixin's came from right there on the farm. We talked quietly during breakfast, the two of us having some guy time before Aunt Lucille came into the kitchen.

After breakfast we headed to Wendell's, a neighbor to the West. He was going to loan us his Farmall C tractor and sickle bar mower. I had been mowing the barn lot and pasture with Clarence's Case VAC and a big rotary mower. Today I was going to learn how to mow hay.

In the machine shed Wendell showed me his mowing rig, a Farmall C with a model 150-sickle bar mower, both were painted bright Farmall red. I thought the C was the most beautiful tractor I had ever seen. I was only 10 years old and in love for the first time in my life.

Wendell showed me how to operate the C safely and how to properly maintain it. Clarence mowed hay with the VAC and I followed him around all afternoon mowing with the C. One of the techniques Uncle Clarence showed me was how to make proper right-hand square corners. There were various ways to make corners. One method involved raising the sickle bar at the end of the swath, making a 270-degree left turn, and then lowering the sickle bar again. This method took up a lot of space and was fairly slow, wasting time. The quickest way was to make a 90-degree right turn while leaving the sickle bar on the ground. If your timing and coordination were good, the corner was square and you never really slowed that much. If you missed, the sickle bar cutters would clog, there would be uncut hay, and it took extra time to get everything straightened out.

Square corners were a difficult maneuver; I was determined to do this well.

The next day I was on my own. I mowed everything in sight, even the road shoulders and ditches. Eventually I got so good at it that Wendell would hire me out to other neighbors who needed some hay mowed.

If you hired out, it was called custom farming. I was a custom farmer and was paid 25¢ per hour. I went from farm to farm at Wendell's instruction. Many years later I realized that these custom jobs were set up specifically to let me earn some money, learn responsibility and develop a work ethic. The reasoning didn't matter; I loved every minute of it. Mowing hay with the C was the best adventure a young man could have.

I liked to mow at a fast speed, full throttle in third gear. This was faster than most. The only time I had to slow down some was on the back twenty acres, as it was full of gopher holes and corresponding gopher mounds. The small front wheels of the C would drop slightly into the hole and then bounce over the mound, causing me to fly up and off the seat momentarily. I hated to slow down, but the bouncing was hard on the C and even harder on me.

Wendell, watching from his pickup, said it was the funniest thing he'd ever seen, me flying off the seat while still holding the steering wheel.

I got very accomplished at performing square corners. Pull the throttle down to half, stomp on the right hand brake, spin the steering with the suicide knob, release the brake, straighten out the steering and throttle up again. If I did it right the mower wouldn't clog, it would take only a few seconds and I was back up mowing full speed.

Wendell removed the muffler from the C and replaced it with a straight stack. He said it was better for the engine. I loved the sound of the engine at full throttle, and the alternating rhythmic swishing sound of the sickle bar blades cutting against the lower cutting plates.

I also mowed oat stubble, timothy stubble and the grass in the waterways; but alfalfa, with a little clover mixed in, was my favorite. I loved the look of the thigh-high alfalfa when it was ready to harvest, the little purple flowers, and the sweet smell when it was freshly cut, as well as the animals that scurried out of the way of the mower, how it fell over the sickle bar, and the pattern as it lay in the field when I was done. I didn't even mind when I got caught in a sudden thunderstorm that soaked me to the skin. I was so intent on mowing, I never even noticed the storm boiling up.

Even though he was thirty years older than I, Wendell and I became good friends. In our spare time he took me to East Lake to fish for channel catfish, and to talk about guy stuff.

I returned to Iowa each summer until I graduated from high school. I never spent a full summer in Iowa again after 1967, but I would visit whenever I could. Wendell and I continued what was to be a lifelong friendship.

When I visited Wendell in the fall of 1984, his health was declining, and he was retiring from active farming. I was worried about him, and I was wondering about the C.

Wendell and I spent the day together. We drove around Osceola and had dinner at his favorite spot. When we got back to his farm I finally built up the courage and asked him what was going to happen to the C. I was afraid all his equipment was going to be sold at auction. My request puzzled him for a moment, and then he said, "Oh, your tractor."

I didn't even try to hide my big grin. We went out to the machine shed to take a look. The C was still the most beautiful tractor I had ever seen. The memories came flooding back from twenty-four years earlier.

"It's yours," Wendell said. "Has been since that summer."

It's now fifty-one years later and the C and mower are in a special shed here at my home outside of Reno, Nevada. I don't have any hay to mow, but I do start her up and drive around the neighborhood a couple of times a year. The straight stack still makes beautiful music. The neighbors all smile and wave and greet me in town as "the guy with the red tractor." The C is like the fountain of youth for me; every time I drive it I feel like I'm ten years old again.

My nephew is coming to visit this summer. It's time to introduce him to the C.

Afterwards, we'll go fishing.

Kent Stephens grew up in Northern California but spent most summers working on family farms around Osceola and Centerville, Iowa. Now retired from a very diverse career in transportation, he and his wife live in Reno, Nevada. He spends many hours archiving family information, stories, photos and movies to DVDs, which he distributes to the family.

HAYING SCARECROW
Delores Swanson

Driving down country roads in the summertime, I often reminisce about the past. When I see a scarecrow guarding someone's strawberry bed or patch of sweet corn, I have to chuckle. I wonder if that's the way I looked in my younger years, while out in the field helping my dad.

Times have changed since the late thirties and early forties. It was not fashionable then for young girls to have suntans, or so my grandmother said, the way it is today.

When I dressed up to help Dad out in the field I was covered, literally, from head to toe. Bib overalls (purchased several sizes too large to allow for future adolescent growth), long-sleeved shirt (buttoned to the neck), gloves to cover my hands and a wide brimmed straw hat. Being dressed in this garb was not exactly my favorite thing, because it was *always* hot at haying time.

My job was to drive the horses on the hayrack while Dad leveled the hay brought up by the loader. Filling the first sling was not so bad. I could climb up on the rack, supported by the ladder in front. If there was a breeze I might catch some of it, but once the second sling was laid on top of the loaded hay, it was different. I ended up surrounded by and covered with the hay piled around me. I have always loved the smell of alfalfa hay, but when I was practically buried in it, that love faltered.

If I want to be totally honest, I probably still would have enjoyed it. Except for the bugs.

The bugs had taken up living quarters in the windrowed hay on the ground. When they were jostled from their beds by the hay loader, and by Dad tossing the hay around, they all seemed to find me. Even as well-covered as I was, the bugs still found their way under my straw hat and even under my collar. I was prepared and had worn a rope belt, but somehow they still found their way inside my bib overalls.

Once loaded, Dad climbed down to unfasten the hay loader, helped me out of my "hay prison," and we headed for the barn. While Dad was fastening the sling ropes to the trip pulley, which lifted the hay into the barn, I would start jumping up and down in an attempt to dislodge my unwelcome friends. When he was finished, Dad would go around the barn where another team was waiting to pull the hay up to the haymow.

My job, when I wasn't doing my "bug dance," was to pull the trip rope when my uncle, who was already in the haymow, yelled. One more sling of hay, and we went back to the field to load up again while my uncle leveled off the hay in the barn.

The next day we repeated the process. Haying always lasted more than one day because we had to wait until the morning sun had dried the dew from the hay.

When I was in my mid-teens years, Dad pulled up in the yard driving a good, but used tractor and baler. It had a wide front end, and lugs on the large rear wheels, but no power steering. Driving our "putt-putt" GP John Deere in front of that baler during haying time created a whole new appreciation for making hay.

With practice, I learned to make nice square corners and never left hay in the field. The memories of being overdressed, hot, and blessed with all those bugs, are behind me, but I still enjoy my open-window drives through farming country during alfalfa hay baling time.

Delores Swanson was a farm girl, farm wife, and a country schoolteacher. She still helps students, through the Foster Grandparent program. At eighty-six years of age, she is still happy to be of service whenever she can.

THE SCAPEGOAT
Marti Ritter

It was a scorching hot midsummer South Dakota day in 1958. My sister Leanne and I had a plan as we dressed in our sun-tanning outfits of short shorts and halter-tops.

At that time our father was serving as pastor to a small congregation in the village of Bijou Hills, South Dakota, as well as tending to our small farm near Platte. Being a straight-laced parent, the only time he allowed us to wear such skimpy outfits was while working around the farm, where the public couldn't see us. On this day he had assigned us the job of mowing and raking in the hayfield, so it was the perfect time to get that enviable tan we desired.

The equipment needed for the job included our small Ford Ferguson tractor, which was mounted with a side mower, and a dump rake that was pulled behind the tractor. The rake had a metal seat mounted above its ten-foot wide span.

The person riding the rake had to sit in the seat and use a foot to trip the lever on the floorboard of the rake, while at the same time pulling a large hand lever to dump the hay. It was Leanne's turn to drive the tractor and mow, and that meant I would ride the rake, tripping the rod when necessary to make long, neat rows across the field of fresh-cut hay.

Both of us were teenagers, with Leanne being sixteen to my seventeen. Ripe with young vanity, we didn't complain about doing this job because we could deepen our tans. We had a reputation for good tans, so much so that our town girlfriends wished they could rake hay.

We put on our suntan lotion, which was a mixture of baby oil and iodine. Sunburn and skin cancer didn't even enter our minds as we hopped on the tractor and rake and began making rounds on the outer side of the pasture.

Things were going well. Around and around we went, making sure the path we cut was straight and the rows of freshly cut hay were all even with each other. We had our thermos of ice water to keep us cool while the sun soaked in. Our black and white mongrel dog, Shep, loped along beside us, occasionally running off to chase a rabbit or two, but always returning to keep us company.

It was hot, monotonous work, but the sweet smell of the hay and the breeze created as we drove along made it bearable.

We were rolling across the field, daydreaming, when suddenly a huge, black and yellow, loudly buzzing cloud rose up beside us. Shocked back to reality, we realized that Leanne had mowed right through an enormous hive of bumblebees that had been hidden in the tall hay!

Screaming, Leanne threw the tractor into high gear as the bees buzzed after us in full attack mode! We swatted at the bees that tried to sting us as we sped along.

I'm sure our guardian angels were with us as Leanne drove the old Ferguson at breakneck speed across the pasture. With the tractor going that fast, the mower and rake bounced up and down, leaving me hanging on to the seat of the rake for dear life. To fall off would have been deadly, because I hadn't had time to trip the rake into an upright position.

Only then did we hear Shep howling. We turned our heads as much as we dared, and we saw the black and yellow cloud chasing our poor dog, bees swarming on him by the hundreds. He howled and yipped in pain as he ran for home as fast as he could. We could see a fading cloud of bees following him in the distance as he ran across the ravine, into the yard and down the hill.

By this time we had reached the edge of the pasture. Leanne stopped the tractor and we hopped off and ran after Shep.

When we arrived in the yard we didn't see him at first, until we noticed something splashing far off in the stock tank. We ran down the hill toward the barn, and sure enough, there was Shep in the tank, swimming around. Bees were floating on the water, and a few were still stuck to his back and nose.

Whimpering, he continued to splash around in the water. Then he slowly crawled over the side of the tank and lay down in the mud next to the creek. Leanne and I ran over to examine him. He had huge welts on his back, and his nose and his eyes were swelling. Poor dog! He'd saved our lives by taking all the bee stings that had been meant for us.

Our mother tended to our few stings. The next day we were back finishing the haying job, donned in our sinfully tiny sunbathing outfits, and covered in our suntan concoction.

Shep stayed in the mud for a couple of days as he recovered from the bee stings. My sister and I loved him a little more after that, for we knew he'd been an awfully smart, if unwitting, scapegoat.

Marti Johnson Ritter, a retired teacher, was raised on a farm near Platte, South Dakota. She enjoys writing, photography, reading and spending time with her grandchildren.

Photo provided by Marti Ritter

Photo provided by Carolyn Kay Koster

BUGSY THE TRAVELING CAT
Carolyn Kay Koster

Growing up on a farm, I knew that cats played an important part in keeping the rodent population down. But to me, an only child, they were my steady companions. Our farm cats, though workers, were mostly tame. I fed them every morning, taking out a tray of leftovers from the night before, mixed with some generic cat food my dad bought at the elevator. The cats were always waiting for me, and I would take a head count: Trixie—check; Fats—check; Squeaker—check; Lucy and Ethel—check; and on it went.

Sadly, I also knew that the life of a farm cat wasn't an easy one. Though my father took care to immunize new kittens as soon as they were old enough, our cats still sometimes succumbed to the usual farm-related mishaps. From cars speeding by on the gravel road in front of our house to the heavy hooves of our milk cows, the occasional funeral was inevitable. Sometimes a cat would simply no longer be there, and we never learned its fate.

Then, one day, a stranger showed up in our yard. He looked to be about eight months old, with gray stripes and a white chest. He also had a crooked tail, and an overly confident swagger. When I approached him he seemed friendly, winding around my legs while emitting a rumbling purr. Liking his attitude, I promptly named him Bugsy, after the famous gangster we'd learned about in history class.

As it happened, the new pastor from our church had stopped by and was in the house, visiting with my mother about an upcoming event. When he and my mother stepped out onto the front porch, I picked up my new friend and said, "Mom, look, another cat. I'm calling him Bugsy."

Mom rolled her eyes. "Another cat. Wonderful."

The pastor looked at the still-purring bundle in my arms. "That looks an awful lot like the cat I just saw at the Harrisons' place, about three miles down the road," he said. "I recognize that crooked tail."

They both stepped closer to stare at the cat in my arms. Bugsy peered fearlessly back at them.

"He couldn't have walked all that way," my mother said.

"And certainly not in the short time it's been since I saw him there," the pastor agreed.

They puzzled this over for a minute, then my mother said, "Maybe he rode with you."

They agreed that had to be it. The cat, as cats sometimes do, must have climbed up into the undercarriage of the car when the pastor had been at the other farm, then dropped down onto firmer ground once the car had come to a stop in our gravel driveway.

The pastor scratched his head. "Do you want me to take the cat back to them?" he asked.

I clutched Bugsy a little closer to me.

But Mom told the pastor not to bother. She said she'd call the other family to let them know their cat was with us, and we could take it back later. I might have protested, but a look from Mom warned me against it. Having had him for less than an hour, I would soon be losing Bugsy.

But that wasn't to be. As it turned out, when Mom called the neighbors, Mrs. Harrison told her that the cat didn't belong to them. It had shown up at their place a few days earlier, they didn't know from where. When Mom explained her theory on how the cat had gotten from the Harrison farm to ours, Mrs. Harrison stated that, now that she thought about it, a salesman had been at their house just a short while before she'd first noticed the cat in the yard.

She also didn't want it back. They had enough cats.

So Bugsy stayed with us, and became friends with Trixie, Fats, et al. For a while, anyway.

About a week after he'd shown up, Bugsy went missing. I searched all around the farm for him for a day and a half. Then, defeated and fearing the worst, I moped into the kitchen just as Mom was hanging up the phone.

She turned to me. "That was Alice Lange. A gray and white cat has shown up at their place. Jodie says it's your cat."

Jodie Lange was in my grade at school. She'd been over to play a couple of days earlier, and she'd met Bugsy. But the Langes lived nearly six miles from us. Mom and I stared at each other for a moment, then I said, "Did you ask Mrs. Lange if any cars had been to their place lately?"

"I did," Mom answered. "She says the veterinarian was there yesterday afternoon."

And the vet had been to our farm the previous morning.

Mom and I drove to the Langes' place, and sure enough, there was Bugsy. He sat happily on my lap during the ride home, staring with interest out the window. I wondered if he was enjoying what had to be a more comfortable ride, or plotting his next expedition.

And sure enough, a few days later, Bugsy was, once again, gone.

This time we didn't get any phone calls. We didn't see Bugsy again, but I didn't worry about him as much as I might have. He seemed to know what he wanted.

He had places to go and things to see.

Carolyn Kay Koster lives in a small town in northern Minnesota, a few miles from the Canadian border, not far from the farm on which she grew up. Even though it's been more than thirty years and she knows it's not possible, she can't help but watch for Bugsy whenever she's driving on the gravel roads.

Photo provided by Terry Overocker

LUCY AND LADY
Karen Jones Schutt

My aunt Lucy, a raven-haired beauty, was the youngest of seven and the pet of the family. She got her way by any means possible, from winning charm to stormy tantrum. Grandpa, however, was not a pushover.

"Papa, I need a horse."

"We have horses."

There were horses on the farm, it's true. They were the big, powerful workhorses with their slow, ponderous gait. Eight-year old Lucy often rode them from the barn to the water tank and back, but that was it. She wanted a faster, more exciting steed, one that would carry her far and wide, maybe even to town, five miles away. To her way of thinking, a riding horse was absolutely necessary.

"But if we had a riding horse I could run errands for you and carry messages to the neighbors. I could get the cows at milking time. I could even go to town to get things for you so we wouldn't have to use the car."

"Lucy, in case you didn't know, there is a depression going on. These are Dust Bowl days, and there isn't enough feed for a useless riding horse."

Lucy didn't see things that way; there seemed to be plenty of feed for the rest of the livestock. She decided she would bide her time and eventually, maybe, get Papa to see things her way. It might work.

Excitement was in the air, one day, when a truckload of range cattle arrived from South Dakota. The truck was backed to the chute and the end gate opened. The men shouted as the wild-eyed cattle jostled each other down the ramp and into the cattle yard. Lucy stood on the fence and added her shouts to those of the men. Grandpa was ticking off the cattle as they left the truck, to be sure the count was correct.

Suddenly, all was quiet as everyone stared in disbelief. Coming down the chute, among the cattle, was a small white horse.

Lucy knew her prayers had been answered. God knew she needed a horse, and had provided one.

Grandpa challenged the trucker, because a horse had not been part of the deal. The trucker claimed he was responsible only for safe delivery. Furthermore, the count was correct. Grandpa, against his will, had bought a horse.

During the following days, Lucy spent every moment she could with the little white horse. She purloined sugar and bread from the kitchen to feed it, and soon they became friends. Lucy named her Lady because she was dainty and sweet-tempered. Grandpa put a halter on the new pet and Lucy began leading her around. They discovered Lady was already broken to ride, so it was only a matter of time before Lucy would give her a try.

Lucy was already a competent rider. Many of her numerous cousins had horses that she rode whenever there was a family get-together, so Grandpa was not surprised to see her riding the horse bareback around the farmyard one day. All the brothers and sisters held their breath as Lucy lifted the horse into a gallop and took off for the pasture.

After that, Grandpa made the rule that Lucy had to stay on the farm. Lucy and Lady explored every inch of it. They carried lunch and water to the men working in the fields and brought in the cows at milking time. They chased the calves out of the garden and generally had a good time kicking up clouds of dust.

Grandpa watched the two closely and observed that Lady was mostly in charge. Maybe she would help curb some of Lucy's willful ways.

He signaled Lucy over to him one morning.

"Lucy, do you think you and your charger could manage to get the mail without strewing it all over the county?"

"Yes!" was her emphatic answer.

Off the two of them flew, north on the gravel road to the mailbox a quarter of a mile away. Lucy had a bit of trouble making Lady stand still while she reached down to retrieve the newspaper from the box.

Because there was no mail, only the newspaper, Lucy had an idea. "Let's go visit Sadie. We'll only be there a minute, and she makes good cookies. Papa won't need the paper until dinner time, anyway."

Lucy kicked Lady's flanks to get her going toward Sadie's house, but Lady had other ideas. She ignored the kicks and headed back home. Nothing Lucy did altered the homeward course.

Lucy didn't know it at the time, but a precedent had been set. From then on Lady never went farther up the gravel road than to the mailbox and back. No display of Lucy's temper ever changed things. However, the road also ran south of the farm. One day Lucy decided to ride Lady down the road to the wooden bridge that spanned Mill Creek. And beyond the bridge was the road to town!

When they reached the bridge, Lady took a tentative step onto the planks and immediately backed up. In spite of Lucy's urging, Lady refused to cross the bridge. She wanted nothing to do with those loose and unsteady planks. Again, she turned around and headed home. Lucy shrieked and screamed, but Lady was oblivious to her tantrum.

Gone were Lucy's dreams of traveling far and wide with Lady, of visiting friends in town, of exploring other country roads. Never would she run errands or deliver messages to neighbors. They were confined to the farm and a short stretch of road, and that was that.

By the time I came along and was big enough to ride with Lucy, Lady was quite elderly. Occasionally she would break into a trot, but walking was her favorite speed. We often rode the quarter mile north to the mailbox and back, and south to the bridge, but no farther. Together we explored the farm and brought in the milk cows. To me this was all high adventure, but I sensed Lucy yearned for the days when she and Lady galloped the length and breadth of the farm.

Though Grandpa had unwillingly bought a horse so long ago, he admitted Lady had more than earned her keep. She had been, for Lucy, a pet, a teacher, a worker, and most important, a soul mate. Lucy and Lady were a one-of-a-kind team.

Karen Jones Schutt is a native of northwest Iowa, where most of her stories are centered. Her works have appeared in the anthologies *Knee High by the Fourth of July* and *Amber Waves of Grain*. *The Callie Stories*, her first book, was released in July 2011.

Dump rake photo provided by Glenn Lynn

Photo provided by Marilyn Kratz

MY DAD'S DOLLARBILL HORSES
Marilyn Kratz

D ad's workhorses were named Billy and Dolly, but he called them Dollarbill, just to make us laugh.

To my childhood eyes, those horses seemed immense, and they probably were quite large. They had to be, to do all the work required of horses on a farm in those days, before tractors were used.

Dolly and Billy had coats of a rich roan color, with blond manes and tails. Their hooves seemed as big as Mom's black iron frying pan. My siblings and I didn't need to be told to stay away from those huge horses. Even though they were gentle and hardly ever made a sound, we respected them as much as my dad did.

Each day when Dad brought them into the barn after a day's work, he'd lift their big hooves and check to be sure no stones had lodged themselves in the crevices. Dad would tell us that a horse with a stone lodged in its hoof would experience too much pain to work.

Dad also curried their coats each day. The horses stood still, seeming to enjoy their daily grooming. I suspect they loved it and my dad as much as my dad loved them.

Whenever Dad approached his horses in their stall, he'd speak to them softly so they wouldn't be startled. They'd make a whooshing sound to acknowledge him, and would stand still as he harnessed them.

Summer was a busy time for the horses. First they had to pull the machines that prepared the soil, then they pulled the planter, and later the cultivator to weed the rows of half-grown corn.

It was usually during the hottest days of summer that the oats had to be cut, shocked, and then thrashed. The horses were probably more tired than the farmers at the end of those long and dusty days.

While we children knew enough to stay away from the horses, their gear was entirely too tempting to us. We loved the leathery smell of the harnesses, and the fly netting provided an appeal my little sister, Donna, and I could not resist.

One day, when the horses were out to pasture, Donna and I decided to play with the horses' fly nettings hanging in a small room in the barn. The nettings consisted of a blanket of long leather strings, which Dad threw over the horses' backs on days when the flies were especially bothersome. The long strings of the netting moved as the horses walked, chasing away the flies.

All those long leather strings called out to Donna and me. We once spent a long, happy afternoon making braids out of them. Of course Dad wasn't a bit impressed with our work. We spent the rest of the day unbraiding!

Dad kept his team of workhorses long after he started using a tractor to do most of the work. But the day finally came when he knew he had to sell them. He didn't talk much that day. I doubt he ever stopped missing his beloved "Dollarbill."

Marilyn Kratz is the author of over 535 magazine stories, articles, and poems, and four books. Her latest book is *Umpire in a Skirt*, a children's nonfiction picture book. She is a retired elementary teacher.

Photo provided by Karen Jones Schutt

Photo provided by Janie Jolene Hart

THE MEANEST HORSE IN THE COUNTY
Janie Jolene Hart

My uncle gave Geronimo to me when I was thirteen. I'd been begging for a horse for years, but Dad always had some excuse as to why I couldn't have one: Unless they're workhorses, they were useless; they're too expensive; I would fall off and get hurt.

But Dad didn't protest when Uncle Al gave me Geronimo, maybe because the horse was a gift, and by then I was tall and strong enough to help with the chores around the farm.

Geronimo was a twelve-year-old quarter horse, with a shiny red-brown coat, white socks and a white spot on his forehead. And from the beginning he let me know he didn't like to be ridden.

My dad told me I had to learn to saddle and bridle Geronimo myself, and that the horse would be my responsibility.

It was a challenge. When I would toss the saddle over Geronimo's back and reach underneath to pull the strap tight, he'd take in a deep breath, expanding his belly. It took me a couple of spills to realize that this meant the strap wasn't pulled as tightly as it should have been. As I rode my horse out from the pasture to the open land surrounding our property, the loose saddle suddenly looped around to his belly, sending me tumbling to the ground. I swore that horse was laughing at me as he galloped off, back toward home. Bruised, I limped after him, cussing my uncle and what I had begun to think was a practical joke he'd played on me.

I learned, when saddling Geronimo, to wait until he couldn't hold his breath any longer and was forced to exhale, then I would pull the strap tight. That solved one problem.

However, it didn't stop him from trying to dislodge me by rubbing up against every tree we came to. I'd have to lift my leg high onto the saddle, out of reach of the tree trunk. Sometimes he'd get just plain mad at me for thwarting his evil plan, and would reach around and try to bite me. Then I'd lift the other leg from the stirrup and out of his reach, so I was perched there on top of the saddle like a frog on a lily pad.

It didn't take long for him to realize that if he chose that moment to bolt ahead, I would go tumbling off backwards.

Again I limped home, using a few choice words that, if my dad ever heard coming from my mouth, would have resulted in a paddling.

Geronimo was also skittish about small animals. At the sight of a startled rabbit darting across the road, or the neighbor's dog, he would whinny, his eyes wide with fright, and dance in place. If I didn't grab the saddle horn I'd end up on the ground again. Even if I did manage to hang on, Geronimo would turn and hightail it back home, no matter my cries of "Whoa!" and efforts to rein him in.

Maybe it was pure stubbornness on my part, or an unwillingness to admit that a horse might not have been such a good idea after all, but I eventually grew wise to all of Geronimo's tricks and managed to stay on the saddle. Once he realized I was not going to be such a pushover, he settled down and we developed an uneasy truce. That's not to say he didn't still drop his ears back in annoyance when I approached him with the bridle and saddle, but at least his open hostility seemed to ease somewhat.

It was during my second summer with Geronimo that he saved my life. We were riding along near the river, about three miles from home, when Geronimo suddenly froze. He stopped so abruptly that I nearly tumbled forward over his neck.

Of course I thought this was a new ploy to get me off his back. When I'd righted myself and felt secure in the saddle, I gave his sides a little kick.

"Don't do that!" I scolded. I gave him another slight nudge, but still he refused to move. "C'mon, Geronimo, I'm not in the mood."

He not only didn't move forward, but he started taking steps slowly backwards. He'd *never* done that before. I was too surprised to even protest.

Then I heard the distinct sound I was well taught to avoid. The *rattle-rattle* of a deadly snake's tail, coming from some tall grass just a few steps ahead of us, directly on the path we'd been traveling. Geronimo continued to step cautiously backwards, until we were far enough away that I could no longer hear the snake's rattle. Then my horse turned and trotted decidedly toward home.

By the time we got there I was as breathless as though I'd run all the way home myself. I hopped off the saddle and ran to where my dad was working on our old car, his head buried beneath the raised hood. When I gasped out my story of the rattlesnake and Geronimo's steps backwards, Dad lifted his eyebrows in amazement and said, "I'm surprised he didn't toss you off right there."

"Me too," I said. We both looked over at Geronimo, who was calmly munching grass a few yards away.

After that I saw my horse in a new light. Though I still had to stay on my guard when riding him, I let him have his way more, allowing him to go where he wanted rather than trying to force him to my schedule. As a result he seemed to relax some, and our rides weren't so much a battle of wills.

Eventually I moved away, and my family kept Geronimo on the farm. When I went home to visit I always made it a point to go out to the pasture to see him, and when I'd saddle him up he didn't seem to fight me so much. Maybe it was just his age catching up with him, but I liked to imagine that he was as glad to see me as I was to see him.

Janie Jolene Hart is a freelance writer now living in Milwaukee, Wisconsin. She grew up on a farm in South Dakota, and kept Geronimo until his peaceful death at age thirty-six.

Photo provided by Roger Stoner

THE FIVE-DOLLAR CALF
Roger Stoner

I had a job delivering newspapers back in 1964. The paperboy who had the route before me had been a little lackadaisical in his delivery, sometimes delivering the paper after school because he didn't get up early enough to do it before. When I started the route, the subscribers let me know right away that they liked to get their papers in the morning, preferably before they had to leave for work.

Another bad habit he had was only collecting the money for the papers every once in a while, at which time his subscribers had to dig up some serious coin instead of just payment for the preceding week. This also made them unhappy.

Both are reasons why I started with only eighteen daily subscribers and twenty-five on Sunday. They were scattered over the full length and breadth of the small northwest Iowa town I lived in, Peterson, Iowa. Peterson runs east and west for about ten blocks along Iowa Highway 10 and straddles the highway with two blocks to the north and one block on the south side. Even with the small number of papers I had to deliver each day, I still had to rise early in the morning, dress for whatever weather conditions Mother Nature was providing, and hustle to get the job done in time to make it to school before the first bell.

My parents, who had heard about my predecessor, agreed to let me take on a paper route with the stern admonishment that I would do the job right and would not cause them any financial hardship because of it. Consequently, my subscribers liked me because I always got the paper to their house early and I collected for the week every Saturday. I had to, because I had to pay my paper bill every week.

I opened my first checking account at the Peterson State Bank and learned how to manage it. It was a good way for a twelve-year-old boy to develop a good work ethic and to learn financial responsibility.

With a population of only about 410 residents, it almost seemed like there were more cats and dogs in town than people. Census takers don't tally the number of furry citizens living within a city's limits, but if they would have that year they would have had to add one more non-human. One that neither barked nor meowed.

My Dad came home from work one day early in the spring and announced that a local dairy farmer, Jerry Dean, was selling his Jersey bull calves for five dollars each. I deposited only enough money in my checking account from my paper route collections each week to pay my bill with the newspaper, and kept the rest in my sock drawer. That was my stash of candy and pop money. But back in those days, candy bars were a nickel and a bottle of pop was only a dime, so I had five dollars in cold hard cash, just lying around looking for place to be spent.

It didn't take much begging on my part to talk Dad into letting me buy one of Jerry Dean's calves. I realized years later that his motive in telling me about the calves might have anticipated that I would want to buy one.

As we drove out to Jerry's farm, Dad reminded me of the chickens we used to raise when we lived on the farm north of town. We got them as cute little fuzz balls, fed them and raised them until they were big enough, and then butchered them for the freezer. He carefully explained to me that this calf was not going to be a pet. I was riding in the back seat with my five-dollar bill in my hand, and while I heard him, and understood what he was saying, I was so excited I paid his words little heed.

When we arrived, Dad told me to stay in the back seat while he went to talk to Jerry. It was going to be my job to hold the calf across my lap when we drove home. In only a few minutes they came back, and Jerry placed the little brown, furry creature across my lap. I held out the five-dollar bill, but Jerry smiled and said, "You just keep that." Jerry and I have been friends ever since.

We lived in a big house just east of the swimming pool, on the west end of Peterson. The house had been built by Gust Kirchner, one of the first settlers in Peterson. It had thirteen or fourteen rooms, not counting the back entry, a pantry off the kitchen, and a back room that opened to the staircase leading up to the "servants quarters." It was a neat old house, with high ceilings and fancy woodwork made from native timber. It has since been made into a museum.

There was also a shed just west and to the rear of the house. It was too big to be a tool shed, but too small to be a barn. So it was either a big tool shed or a small barn. We used it as the latter, and bedded the calf down in a nest of straw. I sat with him, stroking him between the ears until after dark, when my mom made me come in for supper.

Naming the calf was no problem. *Bonanza* was my favorite television show, and while Hoss was my favorite Cartwright, Little Joe just seemed like the perfect name for my little brown calf.

I fed Little Joe with a suckle pail for the first few weeks, until the grass on the slope between our house and the swimming pool started to grow. When the grass was ankle high, Dad put a heavy leather collar around the calf's neck and hooked a chain to it. He put a square, fifty-pound weight out on the open slope and every morning I chained Little Joe to it. Each night I unhooked him from the weight, put him back in the barn and fed him a mixture of oats and corn.

This went on throughout the summer. Little Joe grew so much that by the time school was starting up again, he could drag that fifty-pound weight wherever he wanted to go.

Noting the amount of time I spent with the calf, my mom worried that I was getting too attached to Little Joe. She suggested to Dad that maybe when it came time to butcher him, they could trade his meat for some other beef which might save me grief when it came time to sit down to a steak dinner. Dad said he would talk to the Brees brothers, who were the butchers in town.

Dairy breed bulls are notoriously ornery and have a tendency to get mean as they mature. Dad had never intended for me to raise this calf to the full feeder-cattle size, so he didn't have the calf castrated. Consequently, by early fall Little Joe, who wasn't so little any more, was getting more aggressive with each passing day.

There was no gate on his pen in the barn. There was just an opening, between the second and third horizontal boards, large enough for me to squeeze through. I had to climb through that opening to retrieve his water and grain pans every morning and night, as he always dumped them over and pushed them around with his head as soon as he'd emptied them. He got into the habit of lowering his head and pushing me around, too, whenever I was in the pen. I was a pretty big boy for twelve, but by the time Little Joe was eight months old, I would guess he outweighed me by six or seven hundred pounds.

At first I put up with the pushing and shoving, thinking he was just playing around. But as time went on, his shoves got harder. Finally, one night, he charged me from across the pen and knocked me into the wall. When he backed off to charge again, I dove through the opening in the fence and ran for the house.

"Dad," I said when I got in the house, "it's time to butcher that son-of-a-bitch!"

I think my dad was a little surprised, because there was a rule against twelve-year-olds swearing at our house. In fact, I'd gotten my mouth washed out with soap one time for saying a much less offensive curse after striking my thumb with a hammer. But Dad just smiled and said, "Okay."

I fed and watered the calf the next morning before school. When I came home after school, Little Joe was gone. About a week later, we had some of the tenderest steaks I have ever eaten.

Veal, I believe my dad called it.

Roger Stoner published the *Peterson Patriot* newspaper in Peterson, Iowa, for more than fifteen years. Each week he wrote a column called "Roger's Remarks," which had a large following. Since selling the newspaper in 2004, two of his books have been published: a collection of his columns called *Life With My Wife, the Memoir of an Imperfect Man* and a historical novel about the clash of cultures on the American frontier entitled, *Horse Woman's Child*. Roger and his wife, Jane, live in Peterson.

Roger's calf

Photo courtesy of Kiron Kountry

TRUE TALES OF A QUIRKY GOATHERD
Marjorie Dohlman

Animals are an important part of farm life, and from my experience animals bring a lot of character to a farm. I don't remember any two animals on our farm as having the same personality. That was especially true of the goats that graced our farm throughout the years. The goats were quirky, and they were also one of my favorite types of animal. They got ·me in just about as much trouble as my brothers did.

An unnamed goat that rivaled the size of a mini pony is the first one I recall. He was no ordinary goat. In fact, I don't think he considered himself a goat. My guess is he fancied himself a dog. He wandered freely around, spent ample time on the porch and occasionally trotted after cars arriving in the yard. Obviously, pens were not his style. Neither was a likeable personality. He tended to be a tad bit cranky.

A neighbor boy found out just how cantankerous the goat could be when he decided to prove he was a true cowboy by wrangling and riding it. I have to give the neighbor boy credit, he made a valiant attempt at taming that goat, but in the end the animal came out on top. Literally. The last thing I remember seeing, before I was bent over in a laughing fit, was the neighbor boy running like a track star across the yard with the goat hard on his heels, gunning for his backside.

If I remember correctly, that goat eventually ended up at a new home and became a bodyguard for a herd of sheep.

Sally and Suzie, a pair of Saanen nannies, were the next goats to arrive on our farm. They were a fun and gentle pair, and I loved them from the moment they arrived. They helped me develop my goat milking skills and caretaking abilities. They were the start of a goat herd that got me into some interesting and character-building situations.

A pair of newborn goat kids gave me my first taste of being a new mother. I don't remember the reason the kids were not nursing from their real mother, but I do remember that I was elected their new mommy, and what an eye-opener my goat mothering experience turned out to be! They were a hungry pair, wanting to eat every couple of hours, day and night. I would barely get to sleep when they'd be bawling for another bottle.

The herd was growing, and more goats meant more trouble. One afternoon I was heading out to do chores when I noticed something on the granary roof. At first I thought it was the top of the grain elevator that my dad had recently used to put oats in the granary. As I got closer, however, I realized that it was not the elevator. I couldn't believe my eyes. There was a goat standing on the granary roof.

I figured I had better get the goat off the roof before she fell. Never once did I think about the fact that I might fall off the roof myself. So I hopped onto the bottom of the old-style grain elevator with raised sides, a flat bottom and flanges on chains to pull the grain. Using it for a ladder, I crawled toward the roof, not even remembering that I didn't like heights.

I crept across the peak of the roof, grabbed the goat and pushed her toward the elevator. She definitely resisted my intrusion into her mountain climbing. Once we got to the elevator, I climbed on with one leg hanging over each side. Sliding down the elevator, I pushed the goat ahead of me all the way to the bottom. She valiantly resisted the whole way down.

Once we were safely on the ground, I grabbed my pail and went to the barn to feed the cows. As I headed out of the barn, I saw that same goat standing on the granary roof again. This time I left her there. She enjoyed a few more days on the roof before the elevator was pulled away.

I'm not sure if the roof-climbing nanny was involved in the truck incident, but I suspect she may have been. One summer the grain truck was parked in the pasture. The goats liked the shelter and coolness under the truck and spent a good deal of time there throughout the summer.

When harvest time rolled around, my father started up the truck. On his usual check to see if all lights and such were working, he found that none of the taillights on the truck would light. After checking under the truck, my dad found that the wiring to the taillights was chewed free of its protective plastic coating. I think at that point the goats may have officially become mine.

The billy goats got me in trouble as well. One of our billy goats thought he was a cow. We didn't realize this when we first put him in the pasture with the heifers and the nannies, but we learned quickly. Not long after putting the billy into the pasture, the heifers were stampeding. As the heifers charged by, we saw the new billy goat hot on their tails. After a long chase, I finally caught the billy and kept him penned separately until he realized he was a goat and not a cow.

We later learned he had been raised with dairy heifers at his previous home, and preferred heifers over nannies.

Another memorable billy goat was one that didn't like being incarcerated in a pen. The problem was, he was one stinky billy. He left an unsavory stench wherever he wandered, and his favorite stomping ground was around the house and in the yard. One of his favorite tricks was to jump up on cars that were in the yard. It was not an endearing trick. He eventually wore out his welcome when he chewed up a screen on the house storm door.

Needless to say, the goats went with me when I married. In fact, they arrived at my future home a couple months before I arrived. I later learned that a stipulation to my hand-in-marriage was that there were no returns—on me *or* the goats.

The stipulation didn't bother me. After all, I got to share the antics of the goats with my daughters, and we enjoyed a bountiful crop of apples after the goats did their own special tree-pruning job on our fruit trees.

Marjorie Dohlman grew up on a dairy farm in southeast Minnesota. Goats were her favorite animals in the menagerie that lived on the farm. To this day she still has a fondness for them, and especially enjoys watching new kid goats kicking up their heels in play.

Photo provided by Ronda Armstrong

AND STILL WE DANCE
Ronda Armstrong

Growing up isn't just for kids. My husband Bill and I were in our forties when, in the mid 1990s, we started dancing. Mastering a few basic lessons at a local Des Moines studio thrilled us, even though we knew little about the necessary commitment to stay with it. As novices, the fun and glamour of ballroom dancing swept us off our feet. But not for long. The awkwardness of learning a new skill evoked feelings of youthful ineptness.

Eager to practice in another setting, we headed for the Lake Robbins Ballroom, billed as "The Finest Dance Floor in Iowa," located near Woodward, thirty miles from our city home.

We took the left off Highway 141 onto a gravel road. After a mile or more of fields, farmhouses and horses peering over fences, we glanced at our directions once again, thinking we'd taken a wrong turn. Apparently not, so we continued on.

As we crested a small hill we saw the historic Lake Robbins Ballroom straight ahead, nestled in the lovely country landscape of late May. We eased into the parking lot, staring at the white, unassuming building. No lake in sight; later we heard it had dried up years before. Improvements planned by the new owner and her family had not yet begun.

Dancing in the middle of the cornfields? What had we gotten ourselves into?

Curiosity prevailed over uncertainties. Wide-eyed, we opened the door and discovered a charming world, described by one dancer as "a piece of Americana."

The original wood floor was as magnificent as we'd been led to believe. From the outset, we felt at home. Someone found us a table. Dancers introduced themselves. We slipped on our dance shoes, ready to swing, waltz, and rumba to the inviting music of the live band.

We were inexperienced dancers and newcomers to Lake Robbins. We were also younger than many of the couples we met, who advised us, "Whatever you do, don't stop dancing!"

Their merriment put a lovely shine on their faces and a spring in their steps. We listened to their seasoned advice, as well as the flutters in our hearts. Almost twenty years later we still dance.

Our visits to the Lake Robbins Ballroom were sporadic at first, but we got there when we could, enjoying big band nights and occasional evenings of rock-and-roll. Dance lessons in Des Moines, practice sessions and showcases left us with little time for Lake Robbins, yet the ballroom attracted us with the heartfelt joy we felt when we danced there.

Over time we picked up the history of the ballroom, dating from its opening in 1931 with the Herbie Kaye Orchestra and Dorothy Lamour as vocalist. While some ballrooms closed over the decades, Lake Robbins stayed open through several owners, with a colorful history of bands and performers. We listened to stories from people who had danced there for years, coming from miles around, many traveling farther than Bill and I. Our shared passion for the fun and beauty of dancing united all of us, along with pride in the ballroom's longevity, and concerns for its future.

Work to restore the ballroom to former glory continued, step by step. Bands came and went. The economy wavered. Some dancers found other entertainment, died, or moved, and new ones found their way. After a decade of dancing, Bill and I shifted our focus from lessons and performances to dancing for pure enjoyment. We increased our time at Lake Robbins, recognizing the ballroom had become a valued part of our lives. We also joined several area dance organizations.

Nurtured by communities of dancing friends, our childlike gleefulness grew into firm beliefs about dancing's benefits for health and well-being.

Occasionally, medical concerns resulted in breaks from our routine. Dancing fitness helped our recoveries and led us to the motto: "Dancing through life."

When we retired several years ago, many activities and tasks competed for our time. Drawing on the wisdom of age, we cut many of them, knowing we must, however, not overwhelm ourselves. We saved room for dancing, a joy from our younger years that withstood the test of time. Besides its physical and social benefits, dancing gave us a sense of spiritual unity, a way to creatively express ourselves.

In addition to the Lake Robbins Ballroom's regular schedule, Bill and I continued to look forward to traditional events. Dressing up in festive garb to dance around the massive Christmas tree in the center of the floor highlighted our holiday season. Dances on summer holidays offered food fresh from an outside grill, much like a family barbecue. We helped others celebrate their special occasions and also celebrated our own.

Every November the ballroom celebrates its anniversary. November 11, 2011 marks a milestone: eighty years. Recently Lake Robbins was featured nationally, due to the 102-year-old ticket seller who has worked there since opening night.

Once we had viewed the trips to Lake Robbins as necessary travel to dance at a place we liked. Today we derive much pleasure from the ride in the country. Escaping the city, we observe the fields from planting through harvest, and the bare beauty of winter. Though the city has spread, the still open spaces lure us to a place that has a special hold on our hearts. Every season showcases its beauty; we see it in the landscape and in life.

Bill and I discovered new dimensions to dancing as we grew from eager newcomers to accomplished dancers. The joy of dancing is not the number of steps learned or the execution of perfect patterns. It's the heart put into dancing, it's the spirit set to motion. It's commitment, enthusiasm, and community.

As our years of dancing accrued, we resolved to act as informal ambassadors, to do our part to pass on the fine culture of dancing. Now we're the ones who offer hospitality and encourage others, saying to young or new dancers, "Keep dancing! Enjoy it, have fun!"

Their excited energy invigorates us as we recapture our youthful curiosity, the exuberance of play tempered with our experience. Dreamy-eyed, we wonder, as we observe them, what will these new generations bring? Will they enjoy it so much that they too will promote a dancing life?

Our musings remind us that growing up entails a lifelong journey. As we encounter new life stages, new challenges, ailments or time demands, we take what comes in stride. We make adjustments. We do what we must. And still we dance.

Currently, at barely past sixty, Bill and I marvel at dancers in their seventies, eighties, and even nineties, who continue to step out on the floor at Lake Robbins Ballroom. They inspired us when we were younger; they continue to motivate us now. We dance with the enlightened understanding that dedication, delight, and the pure unbounded joy of dancing brings.

On our first trip, those many years ago, we wondered if we'd taken a wrong turn. What a great surprise to hear music drifting over the cornfields, inviting us to a glorious dancing venue. Today, as our car crunches the gravel and familiar scenery whirls around us, we feel the pull of home, a place where smiles, hugs, and handshakes await us, and music never fails to move us.

When the band strikes up, we hear the spirit-lifting words we long for: "Dance time!"

Joining hands we dance, full of grace from head to toe.

Ronda Armstrong and her husband live in Des Moines, Iowa, with their two cats. Ronda turned to writing after she retired from school social work. Her stories appear in previous Midwest anthologies by Shapato Publishing, *The Des Moines Register*, and several *Chicken Soup for the Soul* collections. In 2011, new stories are forthcoming in *Chicken Soup for the Soul: Inspirations for the Young at Heart* and in *Nurturing Paws*, an anthology for Whispering Angel Books.

SPEAKING OF SHEPHERDS
Deb Kaczmarek

Dad was a genius. But, like many of the gifted boys I would later teach, Dad didn't much like school. Nor did he distinguish himself as a scholar. The dismal grades he earned in literature, composition, arithmetic, penmanship, grammar, and civics must have created some tension with Grandma Jennie. She had been a frontier schoolteacher in Whitetail, Montana, and must've known how bright her youngest child was. Then again, "Chuckie's" grades in deportment and effort may have explained the whole sorry situation. At any rate, it seems unlikely that anyone was surprised when Dad ended his formal education with eighth grade, putting an end to his suffering and that of Miss Imelda Tarbox, the stout and dour teacher of the one-room school near Beaver Creek, Minnesota.

Dirty Joke Telling was Dad's primary genius, though he also had remarkable gifts in mechanics, singing, writing x-rated lyrics, impersonation of professional wrestlers, and mass intake of fluids. We kids were frequently exposed to all of Dad's talents, but none was displayed with greater fanfare and flair than his mastery of stories. He never forgot a joke, and he never missed an opportunity to tell one. Always with gusto.

Dad wasn't particular about his audience. His most appreciative listeners were certainly Mom's twin brothers, Gaylen and Gaylord, both of whom had a keen admiration for the art form but no skills of their own. Dad would just as readily trot out his best material for our visiting schoolmates, which likely accounted for the infrequency of follow-up visits. It was always acutely embarrassing to have Dad perform for our friends. But the mortification intensified for me personally after I assumed the responsibility of bringing my family to Jesus.

When I became Shepherd of the Flock, I was not a legal driver, strictly speaking, so I thought it best to haul my siblings to the nearest House of God, which happened to be the United Church of Christ. It was a humble white frame building located on the same block as the former Greenville-Rossie High School, which had been demoted to serving as the junior high for our recently consolidated school district.

Sue and I took enthusiastically to church-going. I was old enough to join the adult choir, and both Sue and I immediately signed on to assist with Sunday School and Vacation Bible School, in which we enrolled the little kids.

Pastor Dallas Roland was impressed with the Dunn kids. Curious, I suppose, about what kind of family had produced such fervent go-getters, he soon showed up at our house, paying a pastoral visit.

God works in mysterious ways, and I've always believed that Pastor Roland's visit launched me on the path to Catholicism. He was an exemplary clergyman—at least as far as Sue and I could tell as we peered down through the wrought iron floor register that opened our bedroom to the kitchen below. Still, it was a ghastly scene. For the good reverend's visit had unfortunately coincided with one of Dad's drinking days.

Mom was sober as a judge, a condition she may have regretted for the rest of her days. She sat at the kitchen table, helpless, as Dad delivered witticism after foul witticism.

Sue and I broke out in a cold sweat as we listened, but we could not tear ourselves away. I never could remember a joke, so I cannot herein record for posterity any of Dad's gems *du jour*. And I don't remember that our man of the cloth ever got a word in edgewise. Indeed, apart from Dad's raucous enjoyment of his own repartee, it was deadly silent down there.

Tragically, I cannot erase from my memory the view through the register: Dad's whiskey-and-sugar cocktail perched at one edge of the Formica table; directly across from it, Pastor Roland's folded hands, looking remarkably serene except for the rapidly twiddling thumbs.

Soon after this grim episode, I entered the ranks of licensed drivers and began attending the Congregational Church in Peterson. Located at the far end of the county, that church offered the balm of anonymity.

And a pastor who was unlikely ever to make a house call.

Having paid the final tuition bill for her three kids, **Deb Kaczmarek** retired from teaching English and coaching speech to engage in a full-throttle effort to master the flute. It hasn't been going well, so she's branched into writing. Most notably, she collaborated with her five siblings on a cookbook/memoir, a family portrait in cooking oils. She lives in Rosemount, Minnesota, with her understanding husband, Duane, who tolerates her retirement projects so long as rhubarb desserts appear regularly on his plate.

STICK SHIFT 101
Bonnie Ewoldt

I remember my first car like it was yesterday. My parents bought it when I was a junior in college, back in the '60s. Weary of meeting me in Carroll or Sac City or other small Iowa towns between Denison and Cedar Falls, they hoped to make it easier for me to get home on weekends.

When Mom called to say Dad had found a car for me, my excitement went from zero to sixty in three seconds flat! As I talked on the hallway phone on the second floor of Bartlett Hall, I was screaming so loudly that girls came running from their rooms to see if I was okay. I was more than okay—I was in heaven! I was determined to get home that weekend even if I had to hitchhike.

My own wheels. There would be no more waiting for someone to invite me to ride along to Waterloo on Saturday nights. No more begging rides to downtown Cedar Falls, crowding into the backseat of somebody's car, holding my heavy Samsonite suitcase on my lap just to get home for Christmas.

I skipped a couple of classes on Friday afternoon to catch a ride to Schaller, where I met my parents for the remainder of the trip. Watching out the upstairs window that Saturday morning, I saw Dad drive up the lane with the new wheels. There it was, a sweet little blue and white '55 Chevy, my first car. Imagine my excitement as I ran down the stairs, through the house, and down the sidewalk to get my hands on that little beauty.

Mom wiped her hands with her apron as she joined us to inspect my prize.

No rust. No dents. No tears in the dark blue upholstery and no scratches on the dashboard. It was in pristine condition. I was already falling in love . . . and then I saw it. I couldn't believe my eyes. There, on the floor, next to the brake, was an extra pedal. A clutch.

Dad bought a car with a stick shift!

Had he lost his mind? What was he thinking? For as long as I could remember, my family had driven automatics. Stick shifts belonged in tractors and trucks. I had never driven a stick. How was I supposed to get myself all the way back to Cedar Falls the next day driving a clutch?

"What do you think? Isn't she a honey!" Dad beamed.

"Dad got a real good deal," Mom added.

"But, it has a clutch!" I wailed.

Dad told me to hop in, we were going for a spin. As Mom crawled into the back seat, I slowly walked around to the front and opened the passenger door. Stopping me before I sat down, Dad waved his hand and motioned for me to get behind the wheel.

Stick-Shift 101 was about to begin.

Before we started, Dad ran through the fundamentals of shifting gears: neutral was straight, first was down, second was forward and up, third was forward and down, and reverse was back and up.

Or was it second was down and reverse was forward? Did it really matter? My head was spinning and my palms sweating as he rattled off the process: step down on the clutch, turn the key, shift into first, and take it easy while letting out on the clutch and stepping on the gas. He seemed to emphasize, "Take it *e-a-s-y.*"

I adjusted my seat, the rearview mirror, and even the dials on the radio. When I could stall no longer, I knew I had to start the engine.

Putting the column gearshift in what I guessed to be neutral, I stepped in on the clutch and turned the key. To my utter amazement the engine suddenly came to life . . . only to die just as quickly when I popped the clutch.

After a few more tries, I became familiar with the finesse of starting a manual transmission. Step in on the clutch, shift into neutral, turn the key, let out on the clutch . . . *e-a-s-y.* No problem. Why had I been so nervous? This was going to be a piece of cake. It was time to go for a drive!

Vrrrooom. Screech. Vrrrooom. Screech. Vrrrooom. Screech.

Our heads bounced back and forth as the Chevy slowly crept over the rocks on the driveway. I tried to remember if stepping in on the clutch came before or after letting up on the brake—or was that stepping on the gas? Moving the vehicle certainly was not as easy as starting the vehicle had been. I killed the engine every time I tried to shift and go forward.

When we had moved only a hundred feet in a half-hour, Dad threw up his hands, muttered something in German, stepped out of the car, slammed the door, and climbed onto the seat of his Allis Chalmers tractor to go back to cultivating.

After he left for the field, Mom moved to the front seat. Since we lived on a busy highway, she suggested we go to a dirt road near our place, known locally as The Seven Dips—so named for seven little hills in a two-mile stretch.

Reaching the end of our driveway, I checked both directions, held my breath, and slowly navigated the car—still in first gear—across the highway to the infamous Seven Dips.

Though it was safer because of little-to-no traffic, the challenge was greater because I had to learn to shift while driving up and down hills. It was slow going at first. Eventually, however, I understood: first and second going up hills, third going down, while riding neither the clutch nor the brake in the process. As my confidence grew, so did the dust in and around the car as it sifted in through the open windows and billowed up behind the tires.

By the end of that long, hot, sweaty Saturday, I was ready to drive back to Cedar Falls on Sunday. It was the first of many trips with the '55 Chevy. Dad had indeed found a great deal. That car served me well through college and my first years of teaching. My next two vehicles also had sticks, and my husband and I bought sticks. We taught our daughters to drive a stick shift, on a '69 Chevy pick-up truck—but that's a story for another day. I had been converted from being an "automatic" person to being a "stick" person.

Learning to drive a stick is like learning to ride a bike, something you never forget. Recently, I was window shopping in a used car lot. When I showed some interest in a classy little blue and white Grand Am, the sales clerk hustled over to warn me that I would not like it. He leaned over and whispered confidentially, "It has a stick."

I smiled and peeked in the window. Yes, indeed. There was a clutch on the floor. I glanced at the salesman, held out my hand, and said, "Great! May I have the keys?"

As I eased the Grand Am off the lot and headed down the highway, I felt like I was back in my '55 Chevy. Yes, I remember my first car like it was yesterday.

Bonnie Ewoldt is a retired teacher who grew up in the 1950s on a farm near Denison, Iowa She now lives on an acreage near West Lake Okoboji with her husband, Virgil. Her writing ranges from humorous to inspirational, and has appeared in *Country*, and *Country Extra* magazines, and the *Amber Waves of Grain* anthology.

Photo courtesy of Betty Hembd Taylor

Photo provided by Brad Gray

THE WINTER OF OUR DISCONTENT
Brad Gray

"Winter lies too long in country towns . . ."
Willa Cather, *My Antonia*

Twenty-three degrees below zero and it's our neighbor, Effie, banging on the door at 7:00 a.m. "You guys okay in there?" he shouts through the door. "The windows are all frosted over and I couldn't see in."

That would be Effie, checking on these two graduate students from the East who knew nothing of Iowa winters. Or, in his view, much of anything else about practical daily living. He once asked me how I could spend all of my time reading books written a hundred years ago about "made-up people who never even lived."

That was the day the high temperature struggled to reach -3° Fahrenheit by about noon, and then began to fall again, to -21° overnight. And that was the winter the water pipes froze in the ground outside the house and stayed frozen until April.

My wife and I had come to Iowa from the East Coast the year before to attend graduate school at the University of Iowa. We had immediately fallen in love with the small, white gingerbread-style house in Oxford (pop. 705) and were further charmed to learn that the rent was only $100 per month. We moved in at the start of the school year in September.

The fall was mild and the winter no worse than the winters we were used to back in New England. In the spring we spaded up the big vegetable garden in the back yard and planted tomatoes, beans, broccoli, lettuce and zucchini squash. We harvested the stalks from several large hills of rhubarb that grew in the yard, and Effie gave us his recipe for making homemade rhubarb wine, or *piestengel*, one of the original German wines produced in the Amana Colonies just down the road from Oxford. In the fall we picked apples and plums from the fruit trees in the yard, and made more wine using the Concord grapes from the arbor in that abundant back yard of ours.

Life was good. Then our second Iowa winter set in.

Effie—whose real name was Bob, but who had acquired the moniker for his academic performance in school—had seen a lot of Iowa winters and seemed to have a premonition of what was coming. "I'd put 10-weight oil in the crankcase of your car," he said. "Anymore, 10W-30 is way too heavy."

(By then my eastern ears had grown accustomed to "positive anymore," as the linguists call it.)

We never got around to changing the oil and later would pay the price for not doing so. We did, however, have the foresight to pile leaves around the foundation of the house, holding them in place with boards propped up by stakes driven into the ground. Earlier we had mentioned to one of the local farmers our idea of using bales of hay for the same purpose and he, being too polite to correct us, simply said, "Straw would be cheaper."

In the end we settled for leaves; cheaper yet, and abundant.

It was Thanksgiving, and Effie and his family had invited us for dinner, just as they had the year before. I brought along a couple of bottles of *piestengel* to supplement the case of Budweiser Effie always seemed to have on hand.

We stuffed ourselves on the traditional fare, plus a few items I, not being a native, took to be Midwestern variations: cracked corn, yam casserole with marshmallows, and a pheasant that Effie had bagged himself. After dinner we divided into groups of four and played euchre.

In the evening the phone rang. It was Effie's employer, owner of the livestock-hauling company Effie drove truck for, saying that his wife had driven her car into a ditch. Would we go and pull her out?

"Come on," Effie said, "you can go with me. I'll go get the big stake [i.e., stake bed truck] and some chains." He put his coat on and pulled a couple of beers out of the refrigerator. "For the road," he said. "Just in case."

It had started to snow; a bad omen for the months ahead.

By January the cold weather had really begun to set in, with overnight temperatures well below zero. Most mornings we had trouble starting our car, even with the 10-weight oil we had finally put in the crankcase, so we began taking turns getting up in the night to run the engine for a few minutes: the first shift at 1:00 a.m., the second at 4:00 a.m. But some mornings when it was, say, -14°, we still couldn't get the car started.

Then Effie and his sons would come over with jumper cables, pliers and a can of ether and employ their own unique, sure-fire, car-starting method: open the hood; remove the air filter; drop the pliers down the throat of the carburetor, handles downwards to hold the choke plate open; spray in the ether and, *voila!*—the car would start. Usually.

The day the water pipes froze was near the end of a two-week stretch of frigid weather during which the low temperatures were all in the negatives—and I know this is accurate because, with a sort of gloomy fascination, I wrote them down every morning: -5°, -4°, -10°, -14°, -10°, -13°, -12°, 0°, -5°, -11°, -23°, -21°, -9°, and -2°.

The pipes were five feet underground, but with no snow cover the frost had penetrated to that depth as well. Not to worry, said our cheerful neighbor. He'd just get Bill Stratton to come down with his big welder, clamp one cable to the pipe outside on the street, the other to the pipe inside where it entered the house, and run a current through the system until the pipes thawed. Apparently some other houses in town had had frozen pipe problems and this technique had done the trick. But it did not do the trick with our pipes, and many hours later Bill gave up and took the welder away.

(In the spring we discovered that a five-foot length of plastic pipe had been spliced in somewhere in the yard, and the electrical current from the welder was not completing a circuit.)

We hunkered down and resigned ourselves to a long, hard winter: faucets didn't work, car wouldn't start, windows glazed over with elaborate patterns of frost, and sometimes the old gravity-feed furnace in the basement ran 24 hours a day without ever cycling off while the temperature in the house fell degree by degree.

We resorted to hauling water in the car as best we could. We would fill two 22-gallon plastic trash cans at the town pump house, load them in the back of the car and then struggle to get them into the house. We even built a little cart to make this job easier, but on the first attempt the wheels of the cart collapsed under the weight of the load. Twenty-two gallons of water weighs 176 pounds.

Effie and his family were sympathetic; indeed, they were very kind. They invited us to shower at their house, but with six of them and two of us this soon became burdensome for everyone, and we took to showering on campus at the university field house.

The months passed and we gradually grew accustomed to our Iowa winter life without amenities. After all, as in Wallace Stevens' *The Snow Man*, "One must have a mind of winter . . . and have been cold for a long time" to no longer dream of spring's arrival.

And then one day in early April, while we were having dinner, there came a rumbling sound from deep in the basement. Suddenly, with a thunder like a mini-Niagara, rusty water gushed from every open spigot in the house.

About a week later we returned from school one day to find Effie in our back yard broadcasting something on the unspaded garden plot from a five-gallon plastic bucket.

"Nitrogen," he said. "Picked it up at the feed mill. Give your plants a boost."

I looked at my wife and smiled; another spring had come to Oxford, Iowa.

Brad Gray received his M.A. degree in English from the University of Iowa before embarking on a twenty-five year career as an acquisitions editor at Little, Brown, Butterworth-Heinmann and several other nationally prominent publishing houses. Currently a freelance editor and would-be writer working out of his home, he lives in a rural part of Massachusetts with his wife, Virginia, and a large Newfoundland dog, Siegfried.

The house today
Photo by Don Saxton

Photo courtesy of John MacDonald
Nova Scotia Canada

HAL THE SNOWPLOW MAN
Marie Wells

As my friend, Roberta, and I were driving home through Kansas, after wintering in Texas, we were reminded of some of the severe winters in our early years in Iowa. There had been a heavy snowfall across the Kansas prairie the previous night, but on that day, the snow-laden trees and frosted bushes sparkled in golden sunshine.

Along the slippery highway, we saw trucks and cars, like giant beetles, attempting to crawl out of deep, icy ditches. A gigantic snowplow rumbled along ahead of us, assaulting immense amounts of snow.

That plow reminded me of an old, gray, dinosaur-like machine munching bites from windblown snow mounds in the 1930s.

Guiding it from inside of the cab was a personable, pleasant young man with kind brown eyes. We kids called Hal Clark the Snowplow Man. Hal drove this ancient contraption from dawn to dark, clearing rural roads through interminable frigid winters. His routes included the narrow gravel road from Milford, our nearest town, to the county line ten miles west. It traveled past our farm, as well as our rustic one-room schoolhouse a mile away.

If Hal was plowing our road and saw us walking to school, he would stop and call from the high cab window, "Want a ride?"

"Yes," we would chorus as we ran toward the plow. He instructed my three brothers, Dale, Glen and Orville, to hang onto the back end of the machine while I was invited to share the small, warm cab inside. How I, the youngest of six children, enjoyed his undivided attention as we chatted during our trip to the Westport #8 School!

Because the plow didn't come at the same time every day, on bitterly cold, below zero mornings, Dad would drive us to school. Unfortunately, in December of 1932, our 1920 Dodge car broke down beyond repair. Dad's only option then was to interrupt his endless chain of chores, and hitch Prince and Lucy, our big palomino horses, to the sleigh. The sleigh consisted of a wagon box bolted to a running gear. Two pairs of four-foot sled runners were attached to the underside of it instead of wheels. Whenever Dad took us in the sleigh, we would scramble inside and snuggle like little bears under the flannel-lined, black horsehide robe.

Many days we walked the entire mile to school. My brothers had knee high, black buckled overshoes, while my small ones were only six inches high. Wading through deep snow soaked my tan cotton stockings and my long underwear, often resulting in raw, chafed legs.

Sometimes my toes became so cold that chilblains would develop, turning them fiery red, accompanied by terrible itching and burning. No wonder the rides with Hal were so very welcome.

Hal's devotion to all children became apparent on the Friday before Christmas when I was seven. It was during the Great Depression in 1932. A knock on the schoolhouse door diverted all of us from our lessons. Our teacher, Miss Mildred Stouffer, opened the door to Hal, the Snowplow Man, who was holding a grocery sack.

"Is it all right if I come in?" he asked.

"Yes, of course," our teacher replied, mystified by his presence.

With his sweetest smile and his brown eyes shining, he presented each of us with a small paper bag. Inside were pieces of red and white ribbon candy, peanuts in their crusty shells and colorful hard candies, some with soft centers. Also included in each bag was a polished red apple.

What a magnificent treat! Store bought candy was nonexistent at our house. Our weekly twelve-dozen crate of eggs brought less than a dollar in trade for groceries. If Mother got a few cents in cash back, she would walk blocks on painful, swollen feet to save a penny. So there were no pennies left over for candy.

In those days, salaries for workers were meager, often just a dollar a day. Each of us thanked our beloved Hal over and over that day for his generosity.

Those winter episodes with Hal, our wonderful Snowplow Man, are still fondly and gratefully remembered today, nearly seventy-eight years later.

Marie Wells is a retired teacher who taught elementary grades and special education. She still tutors at times. She likes to write about "olden times" so that the current generation will better understand the past.

Photo provided by Marie Wells

Photo provided by Ruth Jochims

LAUNDRY DAYS
Ruth Jochims

When I was growing up in the 1950s, wash day was an all day affair. There wasn't the luxury of an automatic washer or dryer, and our wringer washer was in service every Sunday. Sunday was laundry day because as Seventh-day Adventists, we didn't do hard labor on Saturday. Also, my mother worked, so Sunday was the only day laundry could be done.

Mom was nice and would let me sleep later on Sunday, but if I wasn't awake by nine, she would call to me to get up. If I didn't respond, she sent Midnight, our cat, up the stairs to my bedroom.

If Dad was home, sometimes he sang from the bottom of the stairs, "Can't get them up, can't get them up, can't get them up in the morning—porky, porky, porky beans!"

If that failed to rouse me, Mom had a remedy that never failed. She would come upstairs and throw the covers back. When I finally got downstairs, my two sisters were busy running clothes through the wringer. Everyone else had already eaten, so after a bowl of cold cereal, it was my turn to help.

The washing was done in the kitchen. There were two rinse tubs; one tub was filled with bluing water, which made the clothes brighter. As I ran the clothes through the wringer, Mom cautioned me not to get my fingers caught in the rollers. I ran the clothes from the soapy water to one rinse tub, and then ran the clothes through the wringer into the other tub. Then I took a basket of clothes outside to the clothesline.

I didn't mind hanging up the clothes. I often sang as I worked. One time I put my kitten in the clothespin bag and took its picture as it hung on the clothesline.

Mom made her own starch, and after the clothes were taken off of the line, she dipped the clothes to be ironed in the starch mixture, rolling them up in a damp cloth until ironing day. My memories of ironing began when I was very small. I remember waking from a nap to hear the old soap operas, *Stella Dallas, My Gal Sunday*, or *The Guiding Light* on the radio.

Mom would be at the ironing board while the aroma of soap wafted in from the kitchen. As soon as I was old enough, she taught me to iron. I learned on handkerchiefs. There were no tissues for us to use then. All of our clothes had pockets to hold our hankies, as we called them. Mom was particular about how the hankies were ironed. They were folded in two, folded again, and ironed. The same was true of pillowcases. Everything had to be folded neatly.

When the weather was bad, the clothes were hung on racks in the house. This made the house look messy, but there wasn't anything else to do. One on occasion, when the clothes were draped all over, some relatives made a surprise visit. Mom was embarrassed by the mess, but she still put together a wonderful meal. Her company meals were always delicious.

One day, when Mom was ironing, I was crankier than usual. Her intuition told her something was wrong. Dad was working, so she called a cab and took me to the doctor. I had pneumonia.

Mom was a tender, loving nurse. She had learned to give treatments in college. I didn't like them, but I was subjected to hot fomentations, mustard plasters, and a Vicks cloth around my neck. I hated the mustard plaster on my chest. I always cried, because it felt like my chest was on fire. I wouldn't recommend this today, but I also had to swallow a little bit of Vicks.

Another treatment we sometimes had was an enema. When I was young, that was a common remedy for an ailing child. Those treatments were a sure cure, you know, so I had to endure them.

The best parts of being sick were the special meals Mom fixed for me. The kids today might not think much of it, but I loved the hot milk toast with poached eggs, custard and Jell-O. Sometimes Mom made eggnog, and we always had hot lemonade.

One day I wasn't sick, but I just didn't feel like going to school. When I told Mom I didn't feel well, she said, "I'll have to give you an enema."

I got well in a hurry. "I'm not sick, Mom. I'll go to school."

"Since you said you were too sick to go to school, you're having an enema and then you can go to school."

Mom turned to my sister, Doris, and said, "Go on to school. Ruthie will be there later."

I never tried to play hooky again.

I often think of those hard-working days when laundry was truly a drudgery. I'm so thankful for modern conveniences. Some people still hang their clothes out because they like to, but that's not for me.

If I could have one wish come true, it would be to have my washer and dryer upstairs, rather than down in the basement. How wonderful it would be not to have to go up and down the stairs. But to accomplish this, some remodeling needs to be done.

As Mom used to say, "Maybe when my ship comes in, it will happen."

Ruth Jochims and her husband, Victor, lived many years in Spencer, Iowa, and are now living in Centerville with their pampered black cat, Bailey. Bailey has been the subject of two published poems. Ruth lives near one daughter, and has another daughter, five grandchildren, one step-grandchild, and one great-grandchild.

Photo provided by Melba Olverson
Graves Family Farm

STOVE, HEAT, WATER, AND ELECTRICITY
Melba Olverson

In our kitchen, we had a Majestic cook stove. It provided heat, as well as cooked our food. The stove had a firebox, an ash box beneath it, and a space on the end where small fuel, like paper and small sticks, could be inserted. The top cooking area was cast iron and had three long divisions with two lids in each division that could be lifted off.

The front two lids covered the firebox, but the whole flat surface was heated and used for cooking. There was a warming oven that was above the back part of the stove, and could be used to keep food warm, or for storage. The stove stood on four short legs, so there was also space underneath to keep clean. There was a water reservoir at one end that held five gallons of water, so when there was heat in the stove, there was also hot water.

A teakettle was always part of the equipment on the surface of the stove. The oven was in the middle of the stove, and had a temperature gauge. There were two racks in the oven that could be set at different heights for baking. The reservoir was beyond the oven, at the end.

We also had a kerosene stove that we used in the summer. It wasn't used for heating. It had a fuel tank at one end that fueled the four burners. The stove itself was about five feet long and fourteen inches wide. There was a portable oven, like a box, that sat on two burners. It took practice to keep the heat just right, so we didn't use that one much. When we did a lot of baking, we used the cook stove.

We had a furnace in the basement to provide heat to the radiators in all the rooms of the home. Pipes connected all of the radiators, and the furnace heated hot water that flowed through the pipes to heat the house. Coal for the furnace was shipped into Raymond by train, and hauled to the farm by horse-drawn wagon.

Water was piped from our deep artesian well into the house and was used in the kitchen and upstairs bathroom. In the bathroom, above the kitchen, there was an 8" x 12" vent in the floor that helped to heat the bathroom. Most homes at that time did not have an indoor bathroom, but my dad always prided himself on keeping up on the latest developments and was very innovative.

The water was also pumped to the outbuildings on the farm. A windmill was used to pump the water from the well.

Electricity for the house and other buildings was first produced by a gasoline engine and twelve 32-volt batteries in the basement. The engine would charge the batteries, which would hold a charge for a period of time.

Later we had one of the first wind-chargers in the area. The wind charger was then connected to the batteries. It usually provided enough electricity to the batteries to hold for several days, but sometimes when the wind didn't blow much for a period of days, our lights got very dim!

Melba Olverson was born and raised on the farm near Raymond, South Dakota, that she talks about in this story. She was the only girl in the family with four brothers, and all worked hard to make the farm productive. She married a farmer, and continued the farm life until her health forced her to move into town. She now resides at Avera Sister James Care Center in Yankton to be near her daughter. At age ninety-two, she still loves to write stories and poetry.

Photo provided by Leslie Means

A PIECE OF UNTOLD HISTORY
Leslie Means

Drive outside the city limits of any town in Nebraska, and you're bound to find it. With a dilapidated roof, overgrown weeds and rotting trees surround it. Weathered farm equipment rests nearby, and rodents thrive on the maze of opportunities.

It's a burden, an eyesore to those who don't understand. But to those of us who have lived it, have experienced it, we know the majestic quality that lies within the crumbling walls. We know it's not just an old rundown farmhouse. We recognize it as a piece of untold history.

I had the privilege of growing up in the same home that my father, grandfather and great grandfather grew up in. Established in 1901, my great grandfather literally built the walls that helped shape my future. Christian Waechter was a young man when he came to America from Germany. It's unclear how he ended up in south-central Nebraska, but one thing is certain, he was seeking a better life.

Christian and his wife Elizabeth had nine children, which included my Grandfather Harold. When the great depression hit, most of the children moved, hoping to abandon the looming challenges before them. But my grandfather stayed. He helped his father work the land, and was eventually able to save the home.

My grandfather and Grandmother Vera lived in that home until 1970, when my parents moved in. My father and mother took over the land and home at that time, and still live there today. The sacrifices and challenges my parents, grandparents, and great-grandparents endured helped give me one of the best childhood homes a girl could ask for.

My father would read to my sister and me each night in the very same room in which my grandfather slept as a boy. I sat at the top of our creaky stairs many nights, listening to my father play poker with his friends or my mother read passages from the Bible with her church groups. Our balcony served as the perfect spot for overnight outings under the stars, a great place to tan in the summer and a launching pad when my sister convinced me to use my My Little Pony umbrella to fly. Needless to say, that adventure didn't end well.

I hid in my closet and wept when I learned of my grandfather's passing, and years later spent hours in that same closet crying over my first official break-up over a boy.

My great-grandfather had long passed before I was born, and I was seven when my grandfather died, so my memories of him are vague. Though I wasn't able to witness their tenacity for our family home, I've seen their dedication live through my father and mother. They take great pride in what was built so many years ago, and have instilled that same pride in each of their four children.

We aren't certain what will happen to the farm in coming years. If I had my dream, the home would stay in our family forever. But, with small towns becoming smaller every year, there's a good chance it too could become one of those rural eyesores.

But please remember, if that day comes, don't drive by with disapproving glares. Instead, take pause in the knowledge that you are witnessing a piece of untold history that meant the world to those who lived it.

Leslie Means grew up on a farm near Blue Hill, Nebraska. She now resides in Kearney, Nebraska with her husband Kyle, and their daughters Ella and Grace. After spending nearly seven years as a television personality, Leslie retired from the business last winter to spend more time with her girls and more time writing. She is a published children's book author, and a columnist for the *Kearney Hub*. She also works part-time as the program director for the Kearney Area Chamber of Commerce. You can find details about her Ella B. Bella children's books at www.ellabbella.com.

Photo provided by Leslie Means

Photo provided by Judy Taber

WALLPAPER PASTE
Judy Taber

The farmhouse our family lived in when I was growing up had no painted walls. Neither did it have paneled walls. It had wallpaper on the walls—all of the walls—and on all of the ceilings. The walls in my friends' houses were all wallpapered too. No self-respecting farm family had painted walls. Paint was for the outbuildings: red for the barn, the cattle shed, the chicken house, the corncrib, and the feed shed; white for the board fence that enclosed the house yard.

The wallpaper that I grew up with was mostly patterned. Occasionally we would have paper with an all-over design that appeared to be a plain color when viewed from several feet away. I remember striped wallpaper in the kitchen in cheery colors of red, yellow, white, and green.

I remember huge white paisley designs on a pale green background in the living room, with a coordinating plain-looking paper in the adjoining dining room.

I remember a geometric print that covered the hall going upstairs to the bedrooms.

And, I remember my favorite wallpaper, which was in my bedroom when I was a teenager. It was a light sky blue with a floral print running through it. There were tiny flowers in purple, pink, yellow, and white, all connected with green leaves and vines. It was dainty and pretty and girly, and I loved it. There were white café curtains that I had made for my two windows, and a blue chenille bedspread that was trimmed with white.

Choosing the color and pattern was fun. My mother and I often did that together. The lumberyard in our town carried wallpaper, and a neighboring town had a paint and wallpaper store.

All of the wallpapers were just that—they were made of paper. No vinyl or vinyl-coated, just paper. So, in the process of choosing, we hoped for something heavyweight, which would be easier to hang. More times than not, though, the heaviest, nicest paper was not in a color or pattern that we liked. We would end up with paper that was a bit lighter and, consequently, harder to hang.

We never chose paper to order from the pattern books. We always bought paper that was carried in the store, because it was cheaper. And the final part of our decision would be whether or not there were enough rolls of the chosen paper on hand. If not, we continued looking.

Finally, the day arrived when we would paper the walls. The night before, we cleared the furniture out of the room and swept down any cobwebs that were present. The switch plates were unscrewed and removed, and the shade was taken off of the ceiling light fixture. Other preparations included setting up the pasting table, mixing the paste, and cutting the paper to length.

Our table was made from a couple of ten-foot 2 x 12 boards. We put the ends of the boards on the kitchen table and propped up the other ends on the backs of the kitchen chairs. The boards were then covered with newspapers.

Mom and I always cut the paper to length. If we had a pattern that had to be matched, we used two rolls of paper and alternated them as we cut. There was less waste doing it that way than if we had used just one roll at a time. We would cut about ten strips and stack them on the table, ready to be pasted.

Mom was also the paste mixer. We used a wheat paste that had to be mixed with warm water. She used an eggbeater to mix it and prided herself on having a smooth mixture without any lumps.

At this point, my grandma would take over and apply the paste to the paper with a big brush. My dad and I were the paperhangers. We always had to start with the ceilings. White ceiling paper was notoriously thin and oftentimes our fingers would poke through. We would be left standing on chairs with the wet sticky paper on our heads. Those were some of the few times I heard four-letter words coming from my dad.

Once the ceiling was done, we started on the walls. As we progressed around the room, the brightness and cleanliness of the new paper was inspiring. It was looking good!

Mom fixed our noon dinner between mixing batches of paste and cutting more paper. After eating, we were back at it, and soon we would be done.

We washed the switch plates and put them back on, moved the furniture back in, and the room looked wonderful.

The wet, sticky newspapers were rolled up off of the pasting table and taken outside to dry and then to be burned. The boards were taken back to the basement, where they were stored on top of the braces of the floor joists. There they were reasonably safe from being used as fencing in the cattle lot.

Dad went out to do chores, Mom started fixing supper, and Grandma left for her own house in town.

Another day was done, and we were tired. As we gave the room one last look, we couldn't help but notice that the wallpaper in the next room sure looked dingy in comparison.

Hmmmm!

Judy Taber, a retired adjunct university professor, and her husband, Gary, live in a home that they built on the south shore of Silver Lake at Lake Park, Iowa. Depending on the season and/or weather, she can be found working in her extensive gardens or creating stained and fused glass art.

Photo provided by Judy Hintze

A BARN MEMORY X 2
Judy Hintze

It was big. And it was always RED. It was my favorite subject to draw in the second grade. I would put the blank 9 x 12 paper lengthwise on my desktop, then I would begin in the upper left-hand corner by making an upside down V.

The sides of the mark were about four inches long. The top of it was an inch from the top of the paper. I would take my pencil and draw a straight line from the top, about seven inches long, and then draw a slanted line down. Then I drew straight back to the end of the right side—and there was the roof!

Next, I drew from the left side down to the bottom of the page, all across the bottom and up to meet the edge of the roof. My barn had its shape!

I drew in the haymow doors, windows, and several side doors. A black or brown crayon was my choice to carefully outline the barn shape, all the windows and doors, and to color in the roof.

Then I filled in the rest with the red crayon. That was the most important part. Sometimes I added grass and flowers at the bottom of the picture.

There was a real barn in my life. It was on the farm where I spent my childhood in southwestern Minnesota. It dominated the west side of our farmyard. I remember it as being white, though very old black and white photographs show it as dark in color, which I presume was red.

My mother liked the appearance of white, bright buildings, and diligently painted, with some help, every summer until all the farmyard buildings were white.

According to the land abstract, the farmland on which the barn was built came into the possession of the Southern Minnesota Railroad Company as a land grant around 1869. The railroad later sold some of this land. The barn was probably built in the 1880s. It appeared, due to boarded-over windows and the neatly put together inside walls, that an early owner may have lived in the north end of the barn when it was first built.

In some European countries, the family dwelling was attached to the barn, and that custom may have come with the immigrants to Minnesota. The land passed through a number of owners before my father's grandfather purchased it in 1898. But it was my father's parents who came to live there sometime after their marriage in 1908.

They came from southern Iowa. I grew up in the house that they had lived in, which was remodeled in 1939 when electricity and indoor plumbing came to our farm. In 1935, my father enlarged the barn with an addition on the south end of it. There were lightning rods on the barn roof, which made me think of tall arrows pointing to the sky with a glass ball in the center. From the rod, a grounding wire ran down the roof and sidewalls of the barn, and then into the ground. If lightning struck the rod, the charge would harmlessly follow the wire into the ground. The ball would break if lightning struck the rod, an indication that the roof, grounding wire, and building needed to be checked for possible damage.

My description begins on the south end of the barn, where there was an area that housed our riding horse in the winter. There was a fenced-in yard on the west side of the barn, so the horse and cattle could be outside when the winter weather permitted. In the summer, the horse and cattle were out in the pasture.

Our riding horse was named Midnight. She was a beautiful black horse with a white star on her forehead. The lane ran along the cattle yard fence line, and Midnight would be there when we walked up the lane from the school bus in the afternoon. I would go to the granary and get some oats or ear corn to feed her. She was there waiting for us every afternoon!

Just north of Midnight's area in the barn was a walkway to the inside west wall. A ladder nailed to the wall enabled a person to climb up through an opening and into the haymow. The haymow was like a second story in the barn. Its wooden floor ran the complete length and width of the barn. It was there that hay and straw were stored.

In the summer, the bales of clover hay and oats straw were brought up through the opened haymow doors at each end of the barn. There was a rope and pulley system that brought the bales up off the hayrack to the top of the open haymow door. They were then pulled into the barn and released to fall to the floor of the haymow. The bales were next stacked—a very hot and dusty job in the summer.

The hay was used as feed and the straw as bedding for the horse and cattle in the wintertime. As children, we played in the haymow, clearing away a space to use the basketball hoop. My brothers especially made use of that. I remember the bales being made into forts and tunnels. I don't remember ever being concerned about the tunnels collapsing, though one brother recalls falling through the bales to a tunnel below. He was unhurt.

Back on the ground level, just north of the walkway, was an open area for the cattle to be inside during inclement winter weather. They had access to the cattle yard to the west through an open door. A tank outside the barn held their drinking water.

Also just outside was the tall, brownish brick cylindrical silo. In early fall, the corn stalks, with the ears of corn still attached, were cut and chopped, blown up through a chute and then through an opening at the top of the silo. The tightly packed corn fermented, and was called silage. This, along with the hay, was the winter feed for the cows.

The cows were milked on ground level at the very north end of the barn. There were a number of stanchions for the cows, which held them in one spot while they were milked by hand. In front of the stanchions, the feed was placed for each cow so she would be contentedly busy while being milked. I still have my mother's three-legged stool on which she sat while milking.

The farm cats and their kittens would form a circle around the pan of milk to have their meal, too.

My brothers began milking the cows when they were about age twelve. I never milked the cows, but I did wash the cream separator. It had many, many metal disks through which the milk was forced, and which separated out the cream. My mother used a milk pasteurizer, which heated the milk to kill harmful microorganisms. It was then kept cold in the refrigerator, and this was the milk we drank. My favorite use for the cream was to help make homemade ice cream!

Around 1953, there was a rural milk/ice cream products delivery truck that came from LeMars, Iowa. When the dairy products became available by truck, it marked the end of our milking the cows

The barn is no longer there, but if I close my eyes, I can see it clearly. Sometimes I wish I still had one of my red barn pictures that I so proudly drew in the second grade. My grandchildren would enjoy seeing it, as they enjoy seeing the old photos of the barn.

Judy Hintze enjoys sharing her memories, especially with her grandchildren. After growing up with three siblings on a farm in Southwest Minnesota, she went to college, married and returned to farm life. Reading, photography, travel and her grandchildren are her special interests.

Photo provided by Judy Hintze

Photo provided by Marjorie Davis Arp

MOTHER'S EGG BASKET
Marjorie Davis Arp

My Mother's egg basket is perched on a high shelf in our family room. Mother told me that my father had traveled to Arkansas to look at farmland to rent or buy before they settled on coming to Iowa. The basket was purchased during that trip more than eighty years ago. It's well worn and shows signs of its labors. Looking at the basket brings back the memories of my Iowa farm family.

In February of 1930, my mother and father and their four children migrated from Clark County, Illinois, to rent a farm in northwest Iowa, just south and east of the little village of Harris. They had come to farm in an area that was known to have some of the richest black soil in the world. Their fifth child was born in March. Things went well on the rented farm and three more children were added to the family, making a total of four girls and four boys. I was the youngest child, born in 1938 at the tail end of the depression, shortly before World War II started.

The family was involved in church and school activities in Harris. My Father was a member of the local school board. By 1940 they were able to buy their own farm southwest of Harris. My Father was already farming the land of the new farm, prior to our moving there, when he became seriously ill and died two weeks later, at the age of thirty-six.

My mother was with my father at the hospital when he died. We eight children were at home. My older sister told me that the mailman came by our farm, and we all ran out to greet him. He said, "I am very sorry to hear of your father's death."

The news had reached the town of Harris, but had not yet reached the family at the farm. You can imagine the turmoil that followed. This left my mother with a farm to work and eight children to provide for.

The only memory I have of my father is being picked up by him to find candy in his shirt pocket, but I hold on to it as a connection to him.

My two oldest brothers were teenagers and had helped with planting and harvesting and doing the chores, so my mother decided that with their help, and hired help when needed, she could continue to operate the farm. My two older sisters cared for the smaller children while Mother was doing her work.

The older children had been going to school in Harris when our father died. When we moved to the new farm, the younger children attended the one room country school, Allison #8, one mile from our home. We walked to school with some of the neighbor children. I attended kindergarten and first grade there. My teacher was Miss Marjorie Hembd.

When I was learning to read, I stumbled over the word grandfather. Miss Hembd tried to give me a clue and said, "What do you call your father's father?"

My older sister was trying to help from across the room. I responded, "Pop," as that was what we called my grandfather, and I was not persuaded to change my mind.

All of the children had their chores. Even we little children were able to help gather eggs in Mother's big egg basket, and wash them before arranging them into crates to be taken to town to sell.

We welcomed the coming of new baby chicks in the spring. We had to make sure they had food and water at all times. The brooder house was a very snug, warm place to sit, where we watched the baby chicks and played a game of connect-the-dots on the wall. One of the chores I didn't like was shelling corn with a hand corn sheller for the chickens. Invariably an ear of corn would get stuck, which was very frustrating.

While the older boys and hired help did the fieldwork, the younger boys cared for the livestock and milked the cows twice daily. One of the memories I have is of being asked to head off the cows so they would go through the gate. It was just too scary to see those big animals coming at me, and at the last minute I would run, much to the consternation of my brothers.

When the milking was finished the milk was separated. Then the older girls would wash the separator, a big job that no one liked.

The cows were not the only animals I was afraid of. When I was very little we had a pair of big workhorses named Barney and Bill. One of my brothers set me up high on Barney's back. I was always afraid of those horses after that.

We also had a Shetland pony named Sparkplug. Since he was small I was not afraid to ride him with someone holding me in place. The neighbors had a big English sheepdog named Tub, who was as big as his name implies. He was a very friendly dog, but I didn't believe it. Whenever I saw him coming I'd yell, "Hate dog! Hate dog is coming!" hoping someone would hear me and come to the rescue.

In the spring, we helped Mother plant a big garden. I liked the job, and felt very important that I could put a cabbage plant in the hole she had prepared. We also helped with harvesting and canning the proceeds of the garden.

Summer was time for making hay, cultivating corn, and waiting for oats and flax to ripen for harvest. In the fall, when the grain was ready, a threshing crew would be hired. All hands were needed at this time. Mother would get up very early to cook a noon meal for the threshing crew of at least a half dozen men. She was a great cook and always provided delicious meals of meat, potatoes, vegetables and dessert. One time she had baked a lovely two-layer spice cake with a thin glaze of vanilla frosting. She put it in the buffet to keep for the men. When she opened the door of the buffet to take it out it was covered with red ants. I don't remember what plan B was.

In the afternoon Mother would prepare a lunch to take to the threshers in the field. I sometimes took lunch to the field. It was wartime and shoes were rationed, so we only had a pair of good shoes during the summer. We had to walk through the oats stubble barefooted, which really hurt.

On Wednesday and Saturday nights the cream and eggs were taken to Harris to be sold to the creamery. It was a festive occasion for the whole family to go to town. The solitude of living in the country was broken at these times when we could visit with all the neighbors who were also bringing their products to market. We would take our shopping order to the local grocery store while we waited for the cream and eggs to be graded. There the women and children would visit while they waited to be paid at the creamery.

Sometimes we children were given a dime and allowed to go to the theatre. A local piano teacher played the piano to entertain us before the show and during the intermission. The last two shows I remember seeing there were *Phantom of the Opera* and *National Velvet*. Before the movie started there was a newsreel, and we always thought maybe we would see my older brother in it, as he was in the Navy serving in the Pacific. Sometimes we would get an ice cream cone for a nickel at the restaurant as a treat. Once Mom had received her pay at the creamery, it was time to gather the family in the car and go back to the grocery store to pick up our grocery order. Sometimes it was quite late before we headed home.

Mother stayed on the farm until my older brother bought it in the 1950s. She endured the ups and downs of farming, sending three of her sons to the service, and the illness and death of my second oldest sister, who died of cancer at age eighteen on my tenth birthday.

Our mother's strong Christian faith, courage and strength of character were a model for all her descendants. Her bravery in staying on the farm with our family was incredible. She lived to age ninety-five.

Looking at my mother's egg basket reminds me of the hopes and dreams that she and my father had when they came to farm in Northwest Iowa. I think of them as the last of the westward pioneers of my ancestors. My brother still owns the farm, but sadly, among my mother's thirty grandchildren, numerous great and great-great grandchildren, my youngest daughter and her family are the only ones who live on a working Iowa farm today.

Marjorie Davis Arp grew up on a farm near Harris, Iowa. After she was married, she lived in Kansas, Illinois, Idaho, Ohio, and Arkansas with her husband and four children before returning to the state in 1970. She is a retired secretary and freelance writer. Her husband is retired from the ministry. Since returning to Iowa, they have lived near Clarinda and Waverly before moving to Marion.

MOTHER'S SCRAPBOOK

My mother made a scrapbook,
After Daddy died.
We'd get it out and read it,
And every time we cried.

It held stories and poems,
Of others who had suffered too;
It was her way of sharing,
What she had been through.

The poems oft reminded us,
To love one another;
For only God can count our days,
We're here to love each other.

The scrapbook was a lesson,
That someday we might need;
And I'm so glad she made it,
For all of us to read.

By Marjorie Davis Arp

Photo provided by Donna Dyhrkopp Clarke

THE RIDE TO PREPARATION
Donna Dyhrkopp Clarke

In the 1950s, the 125-mile ride south from Spencer to our grandparents' farm at Preparation took a long time. We loved going there, so we tried to behave. It was a trip through pastures and cornfields, with small towns thrown in to break the monotony. No fast food; a bottle of pop if we were lucky, maybe a stop in a little park. Reading made us dizzy. We didn't have the electronic games that are available now so we had to find other ways to pass the time.

As we rode along, we excitedly pointed out a rare field of milo in place of corn. "Milo, milo maize," we said knowingly. We counted horses; not many were in the fields in those days, having succumbed to old age or equine fever, not that my sisters and I knew that at the time. Deer were fun to spot. They were rather uncommon then, so we didn't see them every year.

We loved passing the Burma Shave signs and reading them aloud. It took several signs to display a full message, such as:

> *THE HERO*
> *WAS BRAVE AND STRONG*
> *AND WILLIN'*
> *SHE FELT HIS CHIN*
> *THEN WED THE VILLAIN*
> *—BURMA-SHAVE*

How disappointed we were if the signs were not where they'd been on our prior trip!

More time was spent reading license plates. We each tried to be the first to spot one from a different state. Iowa tags were also fun because they displayed the 99 county numbers, which were numbered in alphabetical order. Ours was 21; our grandparents' 67. Some we knew well: 97, for Woodbury County, was Sioux City; 14 was Carroll, where relatives lived. Others had even our parents joining in: "Let's see, 78—*hmmm*. Polk is 77, so maybe it's Pottawattamie."

We knew most of our counties by the time Iowa history arrived in fifth grade. Of course, then we had to learn them by location, beginning with those in the northwest corner: Lyon, Osceola, Dickinson . . .

Not unexpectedly, we asked, "Are we almost there?" many times over. I used to think that when we reached Goat Hill we were almost there. Of course, that was only near the beginning of our trip. We were already tired of traveling.

Unlike in later years, the route in the '50s hardly varied, due to the lack of good road surfaces. Even then, the last fifteen miles were gravel, which always made us ill until we learned to suck on fresh lemons.

Much of this graveled road paralleled the Soldier River. Its clay banks were very steep, with the narrow river lying far below. At a couple points, south of Moorhead, we were always certain that our car would fall into the river, which continued to erode the loess soil and move closer and closer to the road. We were rigid with fear, but our father just laughed at us—until one day.

No, we didn't fall into the river, but part of the road did, leaving only our lane intact. Our father stopped laughing. A silent bunch pulled into our grandparents' farmyard a few minutes later. Thank goodness we were truly "almost there" when it happened.

Donna Dyhrkopp Clarke grew up in Spencer, Clay County, Iowa. She loved spending summer days on her grandparents' farm in the Loess Hills of Monona County. Currently, she enjoys writing about those times, researching her genealogy, and painting in watercolor.

Preparation was a Mormon town in the 1850s in Spring Valley Township, Monona County, Iowa. In 1899 the first town, long abandoned, was replaced with a new town of the same name, which didn't last very long either. Our grandfather purchased part of that abandoned property, and in the 1920s had his land description changed from the town streets to the typical rural township/range description. The town first disappeared when a disagreement with the leadership erupted over ownership of the land and personal property. That fight was the subject of a court case that lasted several years and was decided by the Iowa State Supreme Court in December 1866, Scott v. Thompson, 21 Iowa 599 (1866).

Photo provided by Rebecca Groff

BETWEEN IRON AND PAINT
Rebecca Groff

Black iron letters welded onto a platform bolted high above the double doors of a concrete block building announced my dad's business to the world from 1949 until the time of his death in 1979:

E.C. Zobel, Proprietor
Lake Park Welding Works

The shop was situated midway between our house on the east end of town and the school my siblings and I attended on the west end. I almost always stopped in to see him on the way home each day. If I observed that he was especially busy some days I'd merely wave as I walked by.

His usual "quittin' time" was 6:00 p.m. One particular evening, after some late practice at school, I stopped in to catch a ride home with him. The familiar blend of welding smoke and greased iron that he worked around every day permeated the air inside that dark cave of a shop as he closed his dented black lunch bucket. He kept his notebooks for the day's completed jobs inside it—never his lunch—and he carried this home each night.

"Come in here a minute," he said. He seemed kind of tickled about something that night. "I want to show you something I made."

We walked over to a small flatbed cart on wheels on which he'd stacked a pyramid-shaped pile of iron pins. They resembled large fat crayons, only these crayons had little iron circles welded on one end of the shank. My eyes popped at the site of the freshly painted layers of John Deere green and yellow, Farmall red and Allis Chalmers orange.

Hitch pins, he called them. Hitch pins were one of those things that get misplaced easily, I came to understand. He'd been cutting and welding a few at a time, accumulating that stack, and finally had them painted and dried, ready for sale. I felt jealous immediately because they were so bright and cheerful and it would have been fun to paint with those delicious Crayola colors.

"Why didn't you let me help paint them?" I asked.

"Ohhhhhh . . . that's okay," he said. "I just wanted to get them done." My dad always was one to just "want to get it done." Once he started on a project, he knew how he wanted it to go and having kids getting in the way wasn't his first choice, which I knew early on. The job was done now, so sulking would be pointless.

"How much will you charge for them?" I asked, staring at the gorgeous pile and imagining a decent amount of money coming from such an impressive display.

"Two for a quarter," he said.

It felt like someone slapped me. "But that isn't enough! They're so pretty—you should charge more for them!" I couldn't imagine why he wanted to practically give away such beautiful iron crayons after he'd put so much time into them.

"Nahhhh." He shook his head, obviously not too worried about it. "Nobody will pay more than that for them," he explained.

I felt so deflated. It was a striking lesson about certain realities for me that day, as I decided people must be mostly cheap, and that my dad—for whatever reason—was unwilling to ask more on his behalf. I'd heard conversations about just that very topic between my parents on more than one occasion—if that's what you wanted to call those particular discussions.

Through the years I observed that no job seemed too big for my dad the welder. Throughout his career he brazed, soldered, molded, drill-pressed, cut, repaired and welded on everything from oil drilling equipment in California to snowplows in Iowa and Minnesota. He fixed problems on his customers' semi trucks, grain wagons and manure spreaders. Pro bono work included fixing bicycles for local clergy or sharpening lawn mower blades for elderly ladies who had no one else to do such tasks for them. He left behind a legacy of decorative hand railings in which he'd cut and positioned the last name initial for various homeowners around town, along with several impressive church bell towers, made and installed to the specifications of the church committees who hired him. In my dad's hands, if it involved iron, it was do-able.

One would think that in working around those big machines all day long, the man would have wanted a break from it in his off time. But it was just the opposite.

Crawling around, under and over those mass-produced beauties fueled his creative side as he studied how certain assemblies worked, or what didn't, gleaning ideas for his own creations—of which there were many through the years—that filled his favorite downtime hobby of *tinkering*, as he called it.

He loved conjuring up his own designs, often drawing templates and plans out of cardboard to see how things would fit together. Through the years he created homemade wheelbarrows, garden tillers, a giant swing set for my sister and me, and a huge robot-looking cylindrical garbage incinerator behind our house, to name a few.

But his true mechanical love was the infamous garden tractor he assembled from parts he'd scrounged or traded for while out on portable welding repair jobs for his customers. This tractor served as our lawn mower and none of us kids ever had to mow the grass because no one else but Dad knew how to drive the thing. Mowing was his *fun* after being cooped up with welding smoke and irritable customers all day long. He positively adored maneuvering that John Deere knock-off around our large yard, strutting his stuff for passers-by who'd pull alongside the curb to watch. Oftentimes he'd shut it off, and the admirers would poke about the mower and stand back and study it while my dad explained his design logic.

And like any good inventor, he was always working to make it better. So when he decided his design needed improving, it was down to the basement he'd go, working on the next version at the Titanic-sized workbench he'd built especially for his *tinkering*.

But the thing about working with iron parts—old or new—is that at some point they will need priming and painting, yet another activity my dad enjoyed in epic proportions. As any knowledgeable iron-worker knows, metals must be primed before they get their beautiful finish coat, and my dad used only one product for this job: silver paint. Actually, I don't even know if it was an official primer; possibly it was just ordinary silver paint. To this day I cannot tell you why he used it, only that I never once saw any flat, rust-colored primer coats on anything that he built.

Painting was messy business as my dad flicked and brushed paint as if the law would be coming for him at any moment. He, of course, didn't want to get his good work boots all spotted up, so he commandeered an old worn out pair of oxfords and christened them as his painting shoes.

Whenever we saw him change into those shoes, the paint fumes—reminiscent of petroleum and car exhaust—invaded from the garage, or up from the basement if it was a smaller project. "The house might smell like paint for a few days," he'd tell my mother. "I've opened the basement windows to help air it out."

My mother would give him that weary, knowing look that said, "You-and-your-paint . . ." She knew the man and his paintbrush were inseparable.

Through the years those shoes were baptized frequently with flecks of silver, red, orange, green and yellow paint.

The day Dad died he was off on one of his mechanical parts treasure hunts for a snow blower he was putting together. He'd named his new mechanical pet, "Nature Eater." February had produced heavy snows and the pathway out to the shed that day was deep and exhausting. His heart wasn't up to the challenge, and Nature Eater was never finished.

A few days after his funeral, alone in our basement, I sorted and washed the last of his work clothes, still permeated with his familiar brand of hard-working sweat. Underneath the pile of clothes on the cement floor I found the paint shoes speckled by his creativity.

The adult voice in my head demanded I put them in a garbage bag and get it over with. But the other voice—the child's —suggested more kindly: *Why don't you hang onto them for a little while? You can always get rid of them later.* The emotional tug of war that evening felt impassable. Death is the coldest kind of cold there is, and the frigid week we'd been given for his burial felt excessive on top of it all.

The adult kept after me: *And what will you do with them? You cannot hang on to every little thing. It's time to start letting go . . .*

I gave in to her and his trusty paint shoes went into the garbage, but every now and then I wish the child had won instead. But even today, John Deere green and yellow, Farmall red and Allis Chalmers orange still hold a little of my dad for me.

Rebecca Groff, a former administrative assistant and now freelance writer from Cedar Rapids, Iowa, enjoys writing from her native Iowa small town upbringing. She currently does freelance work for the *Cedar Rapids Gazette* in addition to developing her own fiction and non-fiction work for publication. Her blog on a writer's perspective can be found at http://rebeccasnotepad.wordpress.com, and she is on Facebook at www.Facebook.com/Rebecca.Groff.

Photo provided by Cindy Reynolds

HEARTWARMING HOLIDAYS IN THE HEARTLAND
Cindy Reynolds

Holidays in my bustling family of seven were much-anticipated times, filled with preparations and invitations extended to others to join our family gatherings. They inspired me, as my job within the family was to set the dinner table and adorn it with seasonal decorations. While my other siblings volunteered for jobs that kept them in the kitchen, I felt fortunate to be separated from the clamoring of pots and pans.

The standard holiday table setting remained the same: freshly pressed linen tablecloth and napkins, polished silver and fine china from the cabinet. Mom gave me creative license with the table decorations, as she knew I enjoyed making centerpieces.

The changing seasons in Michigan sent me outdoors to collect nature's gifts for the holiday table. At Thanksgiving, I would gather acorns, fall foliage, and then pick apples, pumpkins and squash from nature's bounty, to create a harvest centerpiece. During the Christmas season, I would traverse the snowy trails to collect pinecones, greenery and holly with berries, creating a festive display. The Easter centerpiece welcomed spring, as I clipped branches with flower buds, gathered pussy willows, and searched for fallen birds' nests. I loved the Midwestern landscape, and nature provided the gifts for me to collect and bring indoors, to decorate the seasonal table.

As I arranged the finishing touches on the family table, Mom would inevitably say, "Cindy, could you set another place for two?"

I would typically let out a long sigh before squeezing in a few more chairs and moving the place settings closer together. I could be heard mumbling that we were going to be gathered together like packed sardines.

Nevertheless, Mom's mantra would continue, "Invite them and they will come."

For me, that translated into more table setting. If there were friends without family in town, Mom would surely have her antennas up. I recall commenting that at the rate we were going, we would be dining in shifts. That triggered a light bulb in Mom, and the next thing I knew, she was pulling card tables out of the closet. I was not a magician, and inquired how I was supposed to stretch the linen tablecloth to extend the length of these makeshift tables. Feeling like my job was never-ending, I remarked that the holidays were supposed to be reserved for family, a time to bond and enjoy a reprieve from the outside world.

Mom corrected me and said, "We live in the Midwest, the Heartland of America. The holidays are a time to give thanks for all we have by opening our hearts and widening our circle."

Over the years, the holiday dinner table was filled with both familiar and new faces, old world recipes, homemade edible gifts, and individual family stories. In time, I came to look forward to all the different folks who traveled from near and far to grace our holiday table and to be part of a larger family. As they shared their traditions with us, our lives became more textured and enriched by their company. The appreciation was palpable at these gatherings, and could be measured by the smiles and laughter around the table.

My parents are gone now, but their memory resonates with the values they instilled in their children. My siblings are scattered throughout the Midwest. When we get together, stories are shared about our past and present-day family traditions. We have all embraced our parent's example, and each one of us welcomes others into our homes during the holidays.

I continue to let nature decorate our home and invite family and friends over, keeping that card table handy for extra guests. By opening our hearts during the seasons of homecoming, we light a candle, which helps to make this world a brighter one to live in.

Cindy Reynolds lives in the Boston area with her family. She is the author of *The Pinewood Derby*, and has a published essay in the *Amber Waves of Grain* anthology. She also writes a travel column for her local newspaper.

Photo provided by Melissa Leaf Nelson

QUILT OF FLAMES
Melissa Leaf Nelson

Autumn was a magical time when I was a child. It brought with it not just the beauty of the season, but a unique family togetherness through the work we shared. Harvest on any farm is a busy time of year, but it was especially so on the Leaf farm, because with fall came sorghum cooking.

The sweet smell of sorghum wafted into open school bus windows each autumn as we neared our hillside farm. I raced to the house, changed into work clothes, and rushed to the mill to join in the bustle and excitement. Sliding open the door to the cooking room, I entered another world. The steam and heat fogged my glasses and quickened my breath. It was the most exciting room of the mill, where the year's hard work bubbled into success.

Our lives centered around the making of sorghum, from early morning light until long after darkness fell. I failed to recognize what a rare and special life I led until I got older and met people who didn't know about sorghum—people who didn't even know how to spell it or pronounce it; who had never walked in a sorghum cane field to listen to the shushing of the leaves; who had never smelled sorghum cooking or tasted the thick sweet syrup that, in my opinion, is better on pancakes than maple syrup or molasses and makes the best cookies and brown bread ever invented.

As a child, I took being a third generation sorghum-maker for granted, but not any more. My grandfather, A. H. Leaf, first started raising sorghum cane and making *Bell's Mill Pure Cane Sorghum* in central Iowa's Hamilton County during the 1930s, at the height of the Great Depression. My father, Paul Leaf, devoted his life to making the best sorghum possible, taking over the family business and staying on the family farm that was nestled along a sweeping curve of the Boone River.

Responsible for the entire operation, my father was everywhere and did everything. Dad planted the fields in the spring, nurtured the growing plants and chopped out the weeds in the summer. In the fall he, along with the hired men, turned swaying fields of sorghum cane into cut stalks, and squeezed them into juice. He then oversaw the hours-long process to cook each gigantic pan of green juice through its golden foam phase into a thick, dark syrup holding a glint of sunlight. My brother Chris loved to tell everyone that "my dad raises cane" but he knew, as did everyone who knew my dad, that a kinder and gentler soul was never born to this earth.

In my youngest years before more modern equipment was purchased, Dad and the hired men used corn knives to strip the leaves off the cane as it stood in the field. With rolled-up sleeves and farmer tans, they chopped down the stalks and trimmed the coppered-colored seeds from the top, their muscular arms swinging in strong and even strokes for hours on end. In the field, they gathered the bare stalks in neat stacks. Dad drove the tractor, pulling a portable press out to the field. Using a pump running off the tractor motor, they fed the cane through the press to crush the stalks and squeeze out the juice into a 400-gallon covered tank on wheels, before taking it to the mill for the hot and steamy cooking process to begin.

The moveable press left mounds of dripping remains dotting the fields. We called these sorghum haystacks "plumy piles." For weeks they stood in rows in the field to dry in the sun, until they turned the pale yellow of autumn cornhusks.

Each member of the family pitched in to help with the many jobs required each day. My mother VaDonna and I, along with a classmate's grandmother and aunt, hired on each autumn to help, spent days attaching *Bell's Mill Pure Cane Sorghum* labels to containers that ranged in size from eight-ounces to ten-pounds. We poured the sticky substance from the spout of a thousand-gallon tank into wide-mouthed tin cans and the narrow opening of small glass jars. We kept a clean rag handy for the inevitable spills.

People came from miles around to buy our sorghum. Customers drove out to our farm, not only to buy their year's supply of sorghum, but also to step back in history and watch it being made. The yard spilled over with cars.

When I was too young to count change, my sister Suzanne took charge of selling sorghum to customers, but she let me turn the crank of our antique cash register to open the cash drawer. It made me feel quite grown-up.

Dad handled the deliveries, taking to the road to sell cases of sorghum to grocery stores, cooperatives, and apple orchard stands in Iowa, Wisconsin, and Minnesota. It felt like an adventure when he let me ride along on some of his road trips.

At the end of sorghum season, and armed with boxes of wooden matches, our family returned to the fields to set the plumy piles of sorghum haystacks ablaze.

Mom and Dad picked a calm night for the burning, even though, as a child, I never gave it a thought. Each year, before we took to the fields, we listened to another lecture on matches and fire safety. My brother, sister and I understood the dangers of fire and we took our responsibility seriously. No playing around with matches, not even once.

We each took two rows and crisscrossed the field of plumy piles that stood as tall as me. I walked across the stubble and watched mice scurry away as I tossed lit matches into the mounds of dry stalks. As dusk approached, each struck match created a new flame to join the other growing fires. Standing still, I watched each fire catch and spread before I moved on to the next. I didn't mind the scurrying mice, as I remembered my pet white mouse, Aunt Sooga, who had escaped into the night. Could these brown field mice be her great-grandchildren?

In the crisp air of late autumn, the acrid smell of coiling smoke mingled with the mustiness of dry soil and the decaying leaves from nearby wooded hills. The fires crackled and snapped. Oak, elm, and hickory leaves murmured, as overhead a flock of geese honked their way south along the river. The earth was preparing for winter and those smells and sounds remain with me to this day.

Row after row, we set fire to the plumy piles. Flames sputtered and grew, danced and flickered in the twilight. When we finished, the entire field was a quilt of flames. Dark topsoil and willowy smoke formed the backdrop to the fluttering red and orange squares. I stood and watched in awe, amazed that we had created such a beautiful sight.

With the field aflame and our jobs done, it was time for supper. No use letting perfectly good bonfires go to waste. We roasted hot dogs, heated beans in tin cans, and made s'mores for dessert. No other picnic ever tasted as good.

Autumn is a time for gratitude for another year complete and for the harvest brought in. Some years were quite lean, but regardless the size of the bounty, as the fires burned and the darkness settled around us, we gave thanks for the harvest. Looking back now, sorghum cooking season was filled with hard work, but it was work we enjoyed and did together. It nourished our love for each other and strengthened our family.

I can still see Dad bustling from place to place, tending to everything. He stayed calm and patient, no matter what the disaster. And he experienced it all: equipment breakdowns, hailstorms, strong winds, stuck tractors, broken bones, corn-knife-sliced legs, a wedding band caught in moving equipment, and the sometimes too-early hard freeze that abruptly ended the sorghum season.

Every year Mom created a poster of one of Dad's memorable sayings and hung it up in the mill. My favorite sign said, "Problems are interesting to solve."

To some people, problems are things to wilt under, to be overwhelmed by or to rail against—but not to my Dad. He took problems in stride and solved them. He called himself stubborn. I call it determination. In his quiet manner, he earned the respect of all.

To this day, I close my eyes and my thanks go with the flames, into the night sky.

Melissa Leaf Nelson grew up on a farm in the Boone River Valley outside Stratford, Iowa. She got her love of sorghum and her patience from her father, Paul Leaf. Her mother, VaDonna Jean Leaf, a freelance writer and author, instilled in her an appreciation of the written word and a love of writing. Her work has been published in *Rosebud, Green Hills Literary Lantern, Black Bough* and *The Red Moon Anthology*, among others.

OH, PIONEER!
Nell Musolf

Whenever I wake up on a frigid winter morning—which, in Minnesota where my family lives, is typically every winter morning—I do two things right away: start the coffee and thank God that I'm not a pioneer.

The Laura Ingalls Wilder Memorial Highway runs near our home, named in honor of the author who gave us what might be the most memorable picture of what life was like for a pioneer family in the latter years of the 19th century. The highway follows the route the Ingalls family took from Wisconsin, across southern Minnesota, and finally ends in South Dakota where the Ingalls settled. Driving over the local stretch of the highway in a car equipped with a CD player, comfortable seats, and most importantly *heat*, I think about the Ingalls and all the other pioneers who made their way from the eastern part of the country, across the middle section, and beyond. And as I turn the heat up a little higher to combat the negative-zero temperatures and icy winds outside the car, I wonder each time how they ever stood it.

"What would Pa Ingalls think about this?" my husband always asks as he points the remote control at our gas fireplace and flames burst to life with no more effort from him than a little pressure of his index finger. Indeed, what would any of the Ingalls think if they could see how different winter is now in southern Minnesota? We don't have to go to a well for water, haul the water back to a house we built ourselves, heat the water over a fire built out of wood we chopped, cook, drink and bathe with said water and then finally toss whatever's left back outside when we're through with it. We don't wake up with snow on our beds that fell through the cracks in the roof at night. And best of all, we have indoor plumbing.

I get exhausted just thinking about what the average Mrs. Pioneer did on a daily basis. Her life had to be hard enough during the non-frozen Midwestern months, with the endless cooking, baking, cleaning, and washing she had to do—all without the help of a vacuum cleaner or microwave or even a Swiffer.

And let's not forget what childbirth must have been like for pioneer women. They typically went through that experience all alone with no doula—midwife—in attendance other than Pa, and definitely not a pain pill in sight. And during winter? Fugedaboutit! I have no doubt that had I been a new pioneer wife during the months of November through April, and my husband and I were wending our way westward, I would have been dropped off somewhere along the yet-to-be-named Laura Ingalls Wilder Memorial Highway with a handful of dried corn and curt instructions to find my own way back to civilization.

Frankly, I don't know why any pioneers stayed in this region. One winter of blizzards and ice storms would have been enough for me to encourage Pa to keep going west. Preferably all the way to southern California, where we could have staked a claim in Malibu while there was still a glut of affordable real estate available.

I suppose it's important to remember that Minnesota was settled largely by Scandinavian and German people, both known for their tendency toward, to put it kindly, bull-headed stubbornness. Perhaps Minnesota reminded them of the land they'd left behind. Perhaps winters here were mild compared to the ones in Oslo or Prague. Or maybe they were simply too tired to go any farther.

I know the feeling. Winter in Minnesota does tend to wear one out, gas fireplaces and Swiffers aside. So why do we stay? Why don't we—okay, I—stop complaining, pack the long underwear and get onto the Laura Ingalls Wilder Memorial Highway and head for a milder climate? Because I'm half Swedish and my husband is half Norwegian, and neither of us is willing to be the first to say, "I surrender!" Because we do have furnaces, microwaves, and Swiffers. And most of all because, when all is said and done, this frozen land is home.

I suppose there must be some residual pioneer stock left in all of us here.

Nell Musolf grew up in the Midwest, married her husband Mark and has spent the past few decades moving from one midwestern town to another. So far, she has lived in Illinois, Indiana, Michigan, Wisconsin and Minnesota. Nell is a regular columnist for *Mankato Magazine* and enjoys reading, writing and spending time with her husband and two sons.

Photo provided by Carolyn Rohrbaugh

SWITCHBOARD TELEPHONE OPERATORS
Carolyn Rohrbaugh

When my sister, Darla Rae, was sixteen and I was fourteen, our dad told us we should find part-time jobs. Darla was old enough to be hired as a telephone operator. I went to work at the nursing home and cleaned houses for family friends. When I turned sixteen, Darla left for college. I applied for her job as a telephone operator and was hired.

The technology for dial telephones was still a few years away.

The telephone switchboard had three hundred jacks. Each household in town had a number, starting with one and going up to three hundred. The telephone operator was hooked up to the board through head sets. When a caller picked up the telephone receiver, a light would appear on the switchboard. The operator would plug a cord into the jack next to the light and say, "Number please."

She then plugged another cord into the jack next to the number being called and pushed a button to make it ring. There were a few party lines in town with two families on them. Their numbers started with the word "red" or "black" and the operator would push a red or black button to ring the correct family.

Rural phones had cranks to ring the operator. There were fifteen country lines, numbered one through fifteen, with several households on each line. When a farmer turned the crank, a metal flap on the switchboard fell open to let the operator know someone wanted to make a call. Farmers had numbers such as 51F15. The first part of the number was sort of like Morse Code. Five indicated one long ring, one was a short ring, two was two shorts, three was three shorts and four was four shorts. The last part, F15, was the line number. To make connections, the operator plugged lines into jacks, and then pushed the switch to give the correct ring. 51F15 meant there would be one long ring and one short ring on line 15.

Everyone on the line could hear the call for a neighbor, and some listened in. Rubbernecking, it was called. The more neighbors listening in, the harder it was for the intended caller to hear. "Get off the line so I can hear," was yelled over the line many times throughout the years.

There were four lines for long distance calls. If the lines were all busy, a caller had to wait for a line to open. Sometimes an operator would make a list, and let each person know when there was an open line. When the caller was connected to the long distance call, the operator filled out a charge slip with the number of minutes they talked and the cost so the bookkeeper knew how much to charge for the call.

It was also our job to blow the noon, evening and fire whistle. If a house was on fire or a cat in the tree, town owners simply picked up the receiver or farmers cranked the crank, and told the operator. We flipped the switch to ring the siren to summon the fire department. Upon arriving at the fire station, the firemen picked up the receiver and we told them what the problem was.

Everyone knew everyone; we only needed to give the firemen the name and they knew where to go. When the siren blew, that switchboard lit up like a Christmas tree. Everyone wanted to know where the fire was. We would tell them, as there was no law against it. They would go to the scene to help or just to be nosey.

Most fires in summer were grass fires started by sparks from the train as it rumbled into town.

We took calls for a few businessmen when their wives, who normally took the calls, were away. Don "Skete" Waggoner had a tank wagon and delivered gas to the farmers. Phil Jordan was the artificial inseminator, and Baumgarten's Funeral Home owned the ambulance. Each of them gave us a box of chocolates for Christmas.

Harold Gillespie's mother was very old. She would simply demand, "Give me Harold," and we knew who to ring. Children would ask us to call their grandmother. No questions asked, we knew who she was. Sometimes a crying child wanted us to find their mother. We had a pretty good idea where to call and would find the lost mother having coffee with a neighbor.

There were times when a number was called and we informed the caller, "I just saw them walk by, why not call back later." We even received long distance calls from people looking for long lost relatives, and we usually knew who they wanted.

Upon entering the door of the office there was a small room for customers to make a more private call. I suppose that was Sutherland's telephone booth.

When a call came for the police officer—he was called the night watchman—we turned on the switch for a light that was located on a pole outside. When the officer noticed the light he'd come in, and we'd tell him what the call was about.

Our father, Harold Gottsch, was the night watchman in Sutherland at that time. Jessie Jensen was the head operator and Kate Peters was the bookkeeper. Jessie scheduled two operators for the times that were usually the busiest, but most of the time we worked alone and could be so busy it was hard to answer all the calls quickly. People, being naturally impatient, would click the button on the telephone to get our attention. That made their lights on the switchboard go off and on. As soon as we plugged into their number they would hang up, and as we unplugged the light would come on again, frustrating both customer and operator. We were required to always be pleasant.

An operator was on duty twenty-four hours a day. Clara Burns worked five nights a week; Alma Mueller worked the other two nights. When Alma no longer wanted to work nights, I started working them. There was a very uncomfortable cot that opened into a bed. We would turn on an alarm to wake us if someone needed to make a call. Whenever it stormed the lightening made the metal country flaps fall open and the alarm would ring. We would close the flaps with a paintbrush so we wouldn't be electrocuted. As long as it stormed the flaps continued to fall, we turned off the alarm and sat there closing flaps with the paintbrush. There was no sleeping on those nights.

I worked as a telephone operator for four years until 1964, when Sutherland updated to a dial telephone service, and the switchboard telephone operator slipped into history.

Carolyn Rohrbaugh enjoys living in the Midwest, particularly Sutherland, Iowa, where she has lived her entire life. Six generations of her family have grown up there. She loves to write about the history of the area.

Photo provided by Grover Reiser

Photo provided by Ruth Hunziker Underhill

THE DOCTOR IS IN!
Ruth Hunziker Underhill

My seven siblings and I were born on a farm near the small Midwest town of Washington, Illinois. The first six of us were born with just two years between each of us. Then there was a space of five years between numbers six and seven, and a space of seven years between numbers seven and eight. My oldest brother and oldest sister had already left home and were on their own when child number eight, our youngest sibling, Ken, was born.

Mom and Dad farmed together, side-by-side on many occasions, and then Mom would come out of the field and cook supper for "her tribe," while Dad and the two older boys took care of the animals and did the evening milking and chores. I can't begin to imagine how exhausted they both must have been by the end of the day, after working so hard without the fancy farm machinery the farmers today have.

Despite all the hard work and raising a family of eight ragamuffins, Mom lived to the age of ninety-six, with her mind still sharp as a tack. Right to the end she knew the names of every child, all thirty-three grandchildren and sixty-six great-grandchildren. Mom had been the oldest of twenty-two children herself, so she'd been around children her entire life.

Mom also used to plant and tend a large vegetable garden, and then can jars and jars of the succulent harvest to use through the winter to accommodate meals for her large family. The garden was a very large plot next to the front lawn. When she worked in the garden, she would oftentimes put a big blanket under a shade tree in the yard and plop little Ken down on it, along with some toys to play with, while she planted, hoed and weeded.

One day I happened to walk out to the yard while Ken was there under the shade of the gnarled old maple tree. He had his hand in a tight little fist, with the thumb and forefinger up to his mouth. When I got closer, I realized he had something clutched tightly in his fist and was sucking on it. Hanging from the bottom of his chubby little fist was part of a big fat green tomato worm. Apparently that fat little worm had innocently crawled up on Ken's blanket, and he'd picked it up and literally sucked the life out of the poor little thing. Yuck!

Another time Mom realized that she hadn't seen Ken for a while, so she asked the rest of us if we had seen him. No one had. Mom became frantic. On a farm there are numerous places of danger for a small child to encounter. We were all ordered to scatter out across the barnyard area around the house to look for him. We looked and looked, and called and called.

Finally, we found Ken inside an old wheelbarrow. After that we told him, "If you ever hear us calling your name, you must answer us so we know where you are!"

Some weeks later, when he again wandered off, we called out, "Ken, where are you?" Pretty soon we heard a small little voice from around the corner of the house say, "Here I are!"

That was our baby brother.

When we younger girls played house we loved to dress brother Ken up in frilly, lacey girls' dresses to pretend he was a girl doll. It worked for a while, but eventually he got old enough to rebel, and that was the end of that game.

We also liked to play doctor with our dolls. When Ken was about four or five he wanted to play our doctor game with us and our dolls. We designated a large walk-in closet in our bedroom as the operating room. We would take our dolls into the closet and pretend to mend their ills and injuries. We had a rule that while someone was in the operating room, no one else could enter.

One day little brother Ken was in the operating room for an unusually long period of time. My sister and I were patiently waiting our turns to use it. We waited and waited to use the operating room for our dolls, but Ken seemed to be in there forever. Finally, I walked over to the door, knocked, and asked, "Are you about done in there?"

A little voice said, "Pretty soon."

So we waited. And waited. Once again I knocked on the door, then opened it a crack to see what he was doing in there for so long. I burst out laughing. There he was, four years old, sitting cross-legged on the floor of the closet, operating on a rather large doll that was resting across his lap. We couldn't contain our laughter at such a sight! We knew right then that our little brother would be a doctor when he grew up.

When Ken was still a little guy, Dad bought a farm in a small town near Winthrop, Iowa. Our older brother, with his own young family, moved from their home in Illinois to farm Dad's farmland in Iowa. Ten years later Mom and Dad moved to Independence, so Dad, in his retirement years, could putter around on his farmland and help our brother.

Ken was about thirteen at that time so he made the move with Mom and Dad, thus ending up in Iowa also. He finished Elementary and High School in Independence. He attended college and then medical school in Iowa. After he began his medical practice, the rest of us jokingly accused Mom of saving all the brains in the family for the last one.

Ken is the perfect doctor, with a gentle, generous spirit. He now resides in Spencer, Iowa, where he serves the community as a well-known physician in the area.

Yes, we knew when we saw him operating on a doll draped across his lap that he would one day be a doctor.

Ruth Hunziker Underhill was born in Washington, Illinois. She has been married to her husband, Stephen, for 58 years; they live in East Peoria, Illinois. Their son, Todd, lives in Michigan and their daughter, Vickee Widbin, lives in Wever, Iowa. They also have seven grandchildren and three great-grandchildren. She has been a published author of short stories and poems for more than forty years, and enjoys expressing her thoughts through words.

Photo provided by Julia Wilson Perez

WHY I HATE JUNE CLEAVER
Julia Wilson Perez

My mother never had an easy time of it. I was probably about six when I first realized that my father was not the responsible one in the family. Dad liked to go off for days at a time, disappearing without explanation, and when he did crawl back he usually looked terrible, smelled worse, and was inevitably broke. Being broke was probably why he came back.

He never held a job for long. He complained that his bosses didn't understand his potential. They wanted him to do menial tasks, which he felt were beneath him. He'd either get fired or quit in a huff, telling my distraught mother that he was destined for better things, and that when he "hit it big" we'd all be on easy street.

So when he finally left for good, when I was ten, it was no surprise to anyone. Mom, as though she'd been liberated, set about making a life for me and my three siblings. She told me that, as the oldest, I'd have to take care of my two younger sisters and our little brother while she went to work.

In short order she'd landed a job in the cafeteria at the school my sisters and I attended. Gordy, still a toddler, stayed with a neighbor and her brood of seven kids during the day.

One of the few perks of Mom's job in the cafeteria was that my sisters and I got to eat for free. This was important, because even with her job, money was tight. There was a mortgage to pay, a rattletrap old Ford station wagon that always seemed to need work, and four children to provide for. Before leaving, Dad had cleaned out their small savings account and left her with some of his old debts to deal with.

On many occasions that free lunch at school was our main meal of the day. Supper was sometimes nothing more than macaroni and cheese. If we were lucky, we might have some bread and butter on the side. If we weren't so lucky, the bread and butter was all of it.

Our grandparents, who lived nearly a hundred miles away in Topeka, wanted Mom and us to come live with them. Mom refused. She was the youngest in her family, and as she put it, "My parents are too old to have all of us underfoot. We'll manage."

When the station wagon broke down again, there was no money to fix it. We kids took the bus, but Mom had to start walking to and from the school every day, in addition to being on her feet for several hours in the school kitchen By the time she picked up Gordy at the neighbor's, got home and tried to figure out some supper for us, she was so exhausted that sometimes her eyes would droop shut as she sat at the supper table.

I did whatever I could to help. I always washed the supper dishes, and made sure Christa, Sharon and Gordy were cleaned up and ready for bed. Mom taught me how to cook. If we had eggs, I'd make breakfast. When there weren't any eggs we had cereal, and I learned to add a little water to the bottle of milk to make it go farther.

Mom never complained, but I could see her weariness. Even so, she was still pretty, and I would realize later with some surprise, not yet thirty. A couple of the neighborhood husbands came around at first, helping out when the front gate sagged on its hinges or the push lawn mower needed to be oiled, but when Mom realized their helpfulness brought with it some inappropriate attention, she sent them on their way with a few choice words that had Sharon and me giggling from behind the curtains.

When Mom decided to go to night school, I wasn't surprised. She'd always had a high regard for education. I did, however, wonder how she was going to manage it.

Somehow, she did. For the next two years she took night classes in nursing at the community college. Three nights a week, if she had money for the bus she'd take it, otherwise she walked. She might not have been able to keep up this grueling pace, but fortunately she met a woman in one of her classes who lived a couple of blocks from us, and Mom was able to catch a ride with her.

I had a reputation in the neighborhood for being good with kids. The mothers saw me escorting Christa and Sharon to and from school every day, noting that they were always clean and well behaved. When Gordy started kindergarten, which was half-days back then, I also took Gordy to the neighbor's and picked him up after school.

A couple of ladies asked me if I'd babysit their kids on a Friday or Saturday night. The money was welcome. Before long, I was booked up weeks in advance, and once a desperate mother tried to bribe me into ditching a prior commitment by offering double the going rate. It was tempting. Fifty cents an hour sounded like a fortune to me. But I decided I couldn't leave one of my regulars in the lurch, and I declined.

When she didn't have classes, Mom sat at the kitchen table in the evenings and studied. I started bringing my own homework there, and we'd sit in silence after the younger kids were in bed, our books open in front of us, my squint of concentration mirroring hers.

At least I thought my squint was from concentration. When the school nurse finally figured out that my headaches were caused by nearsightedness, I tried to keep that news from my mother. We didn't have money for glasses. Of course Mom found out. She still worked at the school, after all.

The next thing I knew, our old Ford station wagon, which had been rusting in the driveway for a couple of years, was being towed away. Mom had sold it to the community college for use in their auto mechanics course, and I got my glasses.

When Mom got her RN certificate, she quit her job at the school and went to work at the hospital on the night shift. She bought a car, negotiated with the town dentist for Sharon's braces, and fixed the shingles on the roof of our house herself.

When I started high school she took me shopping for a new outfit, even as I tried to protest. At the department store I stood and looked at myself in the full-length mirror, in my new short skirt—the latest thing—and blouse. Mom stood beside me, beaming proudly as she straightened my collar. "You've grown up while I was busy doing other things," she said, and her eyes glistened with tears that she didn't allow to fall. "I can't get those years back, but at least I can make sure you have the things a girl needs."

Looking at her there in the mirror next to me, it occurred to me that we'd grown up together.

By the time I was starting my senior year in high school, Mom was off the night shift at the hospital and had been promoted to head of her department. She insisted I talk to the school guidance counselor about college. That's when I learned that all those years, when I'd been turning over my babysitting money to her, she'd been putting it into savings for me. My college fund contained not only my earnings, but a little extra that she'd managed to add to it herself over the years.

I went to college, as did Christa, Sharon and Gordy. After we'd grown up and moved out, Mom dated occasionally, but she didn't remarry. She was asked a couple of times. When I asked her why she turned them down, she said, "I've been taking care of myself for so long now, Julia. If some man tried to tell me how to start doing things, I'd probably chase him out the door!"

Mom learned to change the oil in her car, and when she decided she wanted a garbage disposal she bought one at Sears and installed it herself. For Christmas one year I gave her a new tool box because the handle had rusted off of her old one. Gordy gave her a cordless drill because she kept borrowing his.

Now, at nearly eighty, Mom still lives in that same little house. It's weathered, as is she, but they both retain their dignity.

Not long ago I pulled up in her driveway for a visit, my own granddaughter in the front seat beside me. My mother was up on a ladder, cleaning leaves from the rain spout. Fifteen year old Gracie, named after my mother, called out in alarm, "Me-Mah, get *down* from there!"

"Leave her alone," I said, patting her knee. "She knows what she's doing."

And that's why, to this day when reruns of *Leave It To Beaver* come on the TV and I see June Cleaver cleaning house in her dress and pearls, I always have to turn the channel.

Julia Wilson Perez grew up in a small town north of Topeka, Kansas. Her mother, Grace Wilson, has taken up pottery and sells her bowls and vases at flea markets throughout the state.

Photo provided by Betty Hembd Taylor

Photo provided by Vicky Treimer

COUNTRY MEMORIES
Vicky Treimer

It was the mid 1960s, two years after President Kennedy's assassination, three years after John Glenn landed on the moon and four years before Woodstock. Beatlemania was exploding into the hearts of young girls along with The Mamas and the Papas, The Rolling Stones, The Monkees and The Beach Boys.

I was a child of six, living with my older sister, June, and our parents on our three-generation family farm. My dad, Eldon, farmed, and my mom, Viola, was a homemaker, as most wives were at that time. Our quarter section farm seemed like Grand Central Station at times. Aside from farming, my dad did a lot of welding and miscellaneous jobs for other farmers. The recipients of his good deeds would, in turn, return the favor by helping Dad during harvest.

I respected my dad and wanted to be like him, and one day I told him so. He shook his finger at me in response and told me that he didn't want me to be like him, but to be myself. I just smiled and thought that someday, as an adult, I *would* be like my dad and would cheerfully remind him of this conversation.

I continued to swing in the tire swing hanging from the old oak tree. The pleasant smell of lilacs from the lilac bush close by seeped into my nostrils. Gazing into the grove, I counted the five apple trees, along with a cherry tree and two mulberry trees. When the fruit on these trees was ripe, I would pick the fruit and deliver it to Mom to be baked in a pie or cobbler. Not only was the grove plentiful, but so was Mom's large garden, surrounded by a white picket fence. I enjoyed eating the peapods and green beans, as on occasion I'd walk through the garden or help Mom pick the mature vegetables. Rhubarb was a staple in every garden. Mom always made a delicious rhubarb cobbler or rhubarb sauce. Food was always available, as this was an era when folks had their own produce gardens and raised chickens and livestock to butcher.

Our family took pride in our pork sausage recipe, created by my dad and paternal grandfather. Dad would butcher a pig and we'd mix the sausage by hand. We also made ring bologna. I didn't mind helping with the butchering except when it came to chickens. Dad was in charge of chopping their heads off and dunking them into hot water Mom had prepared. The purpose of this was to loosen the feathers so I could pluck them off. Dad proceeded to give me the dead, wet chicken, holding it by the legs. The stench was unbearable, so I made sure I took a deep breath and plucked fast!

I then passed the chicken to Mom for her to wash and clean. A delicious chicken dinner followed.

Dad also raised sheep. Sometimes a mother ewe would die after giving birth. Dad would bring the orphaned baby lamb on the warm farmhouse porch and lay it in a corner on one of Mom's old wool blankets. Baby bottles were filled with warm milk. Mom showed June and me how to test the milk on our wrist to make sure it wasn't too hot for the baby lamb. Dad would show us how to bottle-feed these precious creatures.

On one occasion, he gave an orphaned lamb to the neighbor's daughter, Donna Kay. Delighted, and with a child's pride, she named the dependent creature Cocoa. Sheep kept the grass in the pasture down, and occasionally a neighbor would borrow them to cheap-mow a pasture.

To move the sheep, our Shetland horse, Cloudy, would lead them down the two-mile, dusty gravel road to the neighbor's. Of course, this required all family members to walk behind the sheep with our arms spread wide to discourage any of them from wandering. We watched them carefully, as there was always one who restlessly desired to wander.

Yellow baby chicks were purchased yearly and kept in an octagon-shaped brooder house. There were several windows in the house to provide light, as well as numerous heat lamps for warmth. The chicks were kept in the brooder house until they were old enough to join the mature chickens. That was also about the time the yellow babies changed from yellow fluff to white feathers.

I'd carefully hold the downy ball of baby chick in the palm of my hand. I smiled as I'd gently pet it, listening to the endless peeps it uttered. I could only wonder what it was really communicating.

Farm animals were interesting to watch. Pigs delighted to roll in mud as a way to keep cool on hot summer days. Occasionally I'd feed an ear of corn to a hungry pig, careful not to get my fingers so close as to feel teeth. Dad designed and built open hog crates. The life of pigs has changed over the years. They are now confined in facilities guaranteed to produce the fattest hogs. The smart animal is no longer allowed to joyfully wallow in the mud.

June and I had a lot of boxed games. Fun, for us, was riding our Schwinn and Huffy bikes, playing basketball, kickball or croquet. Sometimes in the fall we'd rake the leaves in the yard into a pile. Then we'd stand a few feet away from the pile, run and jump into the leaves. We always giggled afterwards. On occasion, the gas man, Clarence, would witness our delight with a smile and chuckle while filling Dad's gas tank.

My dad had a 1937 non-runable Buick west of his shop. I loved to play in it, no matter what the condition. On one occasion bees were swarming inside the car, but I jumped in and tried to persuade June to ride with me. Standing outside the car, she stepped closer and peered inside, only to see the bees. She pointed them out to me. I tried to reassure her that the bees wouldn't hurt her. She didn't believe me.

Before harvest, it was a family project to "walk the bean field." We'd each be assigned a certain number of bean rows on each side of us, and be in charge of pulling weeds and hoeing sunflowers for that specific area. That way weeds wouldn't get into Dad's combine at harvest time.

It also was a time of pranks, as far as my sister was concerned. I usually was walking ahead of her, and after I pulled a sunflower and walked a distance ahead, June would "replant" it, only to then point out that I'd missed one. So naturally I returned, thinking I'd missed it. I figured it out when it pulled up too easily. Fooled by June again. Mom had a good laugh, too.

The farm hosted many family reunions, visitors and friends. The awesome sight of the colored fall maple leaves and the greenest grass was the ultimate invitation to come and bask in its beauty.

As the years passed, the business of the farm mellowed. The cost to raise livestock was overwhelming and unprofitable. Gradually, small farmers only farmed. Any livestock or chickens on the active farm were history. The larger farmer became more successful because he could purchase more grain for a lower price than a small farmer. The price of corn and beans hasn't change drastically in the last thirty years. In 1979, beans were six dollars a bushel.

The homestead will forever retain precious lifelong memories for me. The farm is more than a century old now. My old bedroom, the octagon-shaped brooder house that illuminated peeps of yellow baby chicks—they all bring a smile to my aging face.

The fences that kept livestock in are all removed now. The pastureland where sheep grazed is plowed and used for crops. Corn stalks take possession of the area. The buildings that once housed profitable livestock are used for storage.

But it's funny, as my mature eyes gaze across the farm, I still see myself as a child and the activities that once occupied the now-retired farm. Singing birds rest on Mom's rusty clothesline. They chirp of the beauty that greets another peaceful, country day. Rabbits scurry across green grass under the aged maple tree. Rows of soybeans parade the fields at harvest time.

The cries of a harmonious, hardworking life are such a delight! The eventful memories never retire. They just grow more precious with time.

Vicky Treimer grew up on a farm near Hartley, Iowa, and currently resides in Waterloo, Iowa. She has had poetry published in three anthologies.

Photo provided by Kiron Kountry

Photo provided by Karen Jones Schutt

THE MOST DANGEROUS GAME
Mark Smith

Something was killing our chickens. As the oldest boy on our farm I felt that it fell to me to do something about it. After all, I'd read every *Outdoor Life* and *Field and Stream* magazine Dad owned. I'd passed hunter safety class and had fired thousands of rounds at tin cans in the wood lot behind our home.

Obviously, I had been born for this moment.

I knew from my reading that a successful hunt depended on knowing the nature of your prey. So the question of exactly what was killing our hens was important. Sherlock Holmes never searched a crime scene as thoroughly as I did.

The hens were kept in a pen about twenty feet wide by ten feet across. The pen consisted of chicken wire and two-by-fours, with an entrance consisting of a ramshackle screen door fastened to the two-by-fours and held shut with a piece of board with a nail through its center, allowing the board to be spun to open or to hold the door shut as desired. The chicken wire extended to the ceiling. There were no breaks in the wire, and the bodies had not been taken away, so that ruled out foxes, coyotes, and probably raccoons. Also, the chickens had not been eaten. Everything pointed to a weasel.

Whatever it was had attacked in the dark. On those nights when the heat lamp shone, everything was fine. But on the nights it burned out, in the morning I would find yet another feathered corpse on the floor of the pen.

I went back to the house and prepared for my expedition. I sketched a plan of the chicken pen and my plan of attack, which also involved my brothers. I took the sketch down to the supper table to show Dad.

He looked at it and rubbed his beard. "Suppose you explain this to me," he suggested.

"Well, first of all, I'll have the .22 automatic and I'll be here, at the front of the pen," I said, pointing at a place on the paper. "Dan will be sitting in the rafters with the .410."

"In the rafters?" Dad asked.

"Yes."

"With a shotgun?"

"Yes."

"In the dark?"

"No," I replied happily, "Matt will be holding a flashlight."

"I want a gun too," Matt whined.

"Ok," I agreed. "You can have the single-shot .22. But you'll have to hold the flashlight in your other hand."

"Why can't Dan hold it?"

"Because he'll be sitting in the rafters with the shotgun," I explained in my frustrated-genius tone. "He might drop it."

Dad rubbed his beard again. As he looked at my sketch and listened to me explain it to my partners, he came to a conclusion. If he wanted eggs in the near future, not to mention grandchildren later on, my plan needed revising.

"First of all," Dad said, "Dan might drop more than a flashlight. Not to mention, shooting down onto a cement floor could cause ricochets. So, no rafters. Secondly, you do realize that you'll have three guns firing at different angles in a small enclosed area?"

"The idea is to catch it in a crossfire," I explained.

"I see," Dad said rubbing his beard, "That's what I'm afraid of. You can take the single shot .22, and your brothers can each hold a flashlight."

So it was that the three of us found ourselves sitting in the barn, in the dark, on a chilly February night.

"I'm cold," Matt said.

"Sh-h-h," I hissed.

"I wish Dad had let me have the rifle," Dan said.

"Sh-h-h!"

"I'm bored," Dan said. "How long have we been out here?"

I checked my watch. "Fifteen minutes. Look, we'll stay until nine and then go inside. That'll be an hour."

And so time passed . . .

"Sh-h-h," I hissed.

"I didn't say anything," Matt said.

"I didn't either," said Dan.

"*Sh-h-h!* Do you hear that?"

A scratching sound came from the back of the hencoop.

"Turn on the light," I commanded.

From the rear of the coop, behind the double-layered wall, came the scratching sound again. As we watched, a black furry creature crawled up from between the walls and started to walk back and forth along the nests, looking like a target at a shooting gallery.

"It's a skunk," Matt gasped.

"No it's not, it's a civet cat," Dan answered.

"It's a skunk."

"I can see the spots, it's a civet cat. I read about them in Mark Trail's book of—"

"Hold the light still," I snapped.

Raising my rifle, I took careful aim. My hands were shaking, so I did as Dad had taught me. Stop. Take a deep breath. Let half of it out, then squeeze . . .

CRACK.

Instantly the barn was plunged into darkness as my brothers dropped their flashlights to the floor and ran. I considered my options. My rifle was empty, I couldn't see to load it, and I had no idea if the skunk was dead, wounded, or just plain annoyed.

I followed my brothers out the door.

The next day there was no sign of the skunk. But a wet pair of long johns was found in the bin next to the laundry basket. Matt said they were Dan's. Dan said that "a skunk smells his own hole first."

I didn't want to talk about skunks. But a week later, when no chickens had been killed, Dad looked at me across breakfast and said, "You must have got him. Good job, son."

I never dared confess that the long johns were mine.

Writer **Mark Smith,** in spite of his best intentions, survived into adulthood. He intends to use his handsome payment for *The Most Dangerous Game* to spend on alcohol so future biographers will compare him with Ernest Hemingway—having drunk away his professional earnings!

MY SUMMER VACATION
Linda Ireland

I grew up in Waterloo. Unlike Napoleon, I didn't have to wait until I was an adult to find out how unfair the world can be to those who aspire to something greater. I was doomed from the beginning.

When I was young in the early sixties, Waterloo was a booming town in Iowa. John Deere and the Rath Packing Plant were thriving, and the men who worked there made enough money to be considered rich by the rest of us. Their families had nicely decorated and landscaped homes and yards, and not only cars but also boats and campers in their garages.

My family was poor in comparison. My dad made enough money as a mechanic to keep us fed and clothed, and to keep a roof over our heads, but our house was filled with secondhand furniture, our yard (since we had no garage) was littered with car parts, and I didn't get new clothes for school every year like the kids whose parents worked in factories. We didn't take summer vacations, either.

Summers were different for kids back then. Instead of getting out of school in the spring and going to day care all day in the summer, we stayed home with our moms. Long days stretched ahead; in the spring, it was an adventure, but by fall, it got boring. After three long months with nothing to do, school looked exciting.

I loved going back to school in the fall except for one thing—I dreaded that first essay, "How I Spent My Summer Vacation." In first through fourth grades, I told the truth. After all, those were the years when truth mattered. As kids, if we got caught doing something wrong, the punishment was ten times as bad if we lied about it.

So early on, I told the truth. I wrote essays about how I spent my summers playing softball, riding my bike, and reading books in the top of the willow tree while eating bologna sandwiches on white bread and Hostess Ding Dongs. I wrote about how I played poker on the picnic table with Freddie, who lived across the street. To this day, I can't look at a deck of cards without thinking "Jack of Diamonds, Jack of Diamonds, I knew him quite well," since that's what Freddie chanted throughout each game.

I liked playing cards with Freddie, except he tended to cheat. When he got cards he didn't like, he'd drop them through the slats in the picnic table so he could draw new ones. That made me mad.

When essay-time rolled around at the beginning of fifth grade, the peer pressure from the kids whose fathers worked at factories—and whose families took great summer vacations where they actually left Iowa, while I barely left my street—had become too much for me. I decided not to write an essay that would make the rich kids laugh, and then look at me with pity. I decided to lie.

It wasn't a huge leap. I had already learned the previous year that sometimes you just get so worn down, the truth doesn't matter anymore. Mary Sullivan had cornered me in the hallway at school shortly after fourth grade started and asked me if I liked her new dress. I told the truth: it was kind of ugly. She burst into tears, so then I told her that even though it was kind of ugly, it was also very pretty and I liked it a lot. I felt really bad about hurting her feelings.

Lying wasn't natural to me, though, so first I tried to talk the teacher into letting us write something different this year. I suggested a book report, since I'd read a lot of books in the willow tree that summer, but that made all the other kids groan. The teacher stuck to her guns and gave me a "rah-rah, you can do it" speech. Our summer vacation essay was due at the end of the week.

I worked harder on that essay than any other I'd ever written, mostly because it takes extra time when you're making stuff up. First I told how my family flew to New York City in July and went to a Broadway show where half-dressed "Rocket Girls" stood in a long line and kicked their bare legs high in the air. Then I had us eating dinner in Chinatown, going to the top of the Empire State Building and into the Statue of Liberty's crown, and having our picture taken in Times Square where the ball dropped each year. After that, we boarded a ship at the New York City docks and sailed to Africa, where we enlisted a native guide with bones through his nose and white plant juice streaked on his face to take us on safari, which is when I shot a rhinoceros whose horn I brought home as a souvenir.

I was actually quite pleased with the essay, as I thought it demonstrated imagination and creativity. I decided that when I presented it, if anyone asked to see pictures or the rhino horn, I would explain that the film had been ruined when my sister knocked the camera into the bathtub at the hotel on the way home, and that the horn was in a safe deposit box because it was so valuable. I thought that showed a strong ability to plan for the future.

When presentation day came, I wore my best dress and had my brother's girlfriend rat and comb my hair into a French twist, so I'd look like a sophisticated, well-traveled lady.

I was so excited about sharing my adventures with the class. When my turn came, I read my essay in a voice that combined the enthusiasm of seeing new places with the blasé attitude one develops once one has done so. I thought it went very well; the students' *oohs* and *ahhhs*, particularly during the safari descriptions, were very satisfying.

At the end of class, however, everything changed, much as it must have done for Napoleon when he rode into Waterloo with stars in his eyes. As the teacher handed back the essays, I pictured a large red A and a comment like "Incredible work" in the upper corner of the page. That was back in the days when teachers corrected essays, and thought nothing of scribbling all over them in red pencil, since they labored under the assumption that teaching grammar and punctuation, so a student could write in a way that could be understood, was a good thing.

Imagine my shock when I saw nothing on my paper but a large note at the bottom saying, "See me after class. We're going to the principal's office."

I told myself it was probably nothing, that maybe she'd enjoyed the story so much she wanted to make a copy of it for the principal on the machine in his office. But deep inside, I knew that wasn't the case. This was confirmed when, as the teacher and I strode down the right side of the hallway after class, I saw my mother waiting outside the principal's door.

My teacher, my mother, and I had to wait for a while on the bench outside the door. We sat there, three grim faces perched over three slumped bodies, with the smallest being the most grim and slumped, until the principal called us into his room.

While we waited, I tried to figure out whether I could convince my mom that some other kid wrote that paper and put my name on it. But no, I had just read it in class—that wouldn't work. I decided my best bet would be to claim that I didn't understand the assignment, and hope the teacher would forget to mention that I'd completed it accurately the previous four years.

Finally the principal called us in and offered us chairs across the desk from him. That was before people in power found out that it's better to sit at round tables or in a circle so everyone will feel equal. It was also before principals discovered that they shouldn't stand behind their desks and yell at students, and then send them away with parents who got to decide what punishment was warranted. After what seemed to be a year of yelling, sprinkled with references to the Ten Commandments, and to one in particular, I was sent home with my mother, who promptly took away my TV privileges, sent me to my room, and told me to just wait until my father got home.

I tried to explain to my mother how in some situations the truth just doesn't matter, but she wasn't buying it. A couple of weeks later, however, I was proven correct. Late one afternoon at the picnic table, before Freddie and I started our poker game, I read my essay to him. He listened, obviously enraptured, and afterward gazed at me with new respect in his eyes. I had little trouble with him cheating at cards after that.

So to this day, I still maintain that, no matter what that principal, teacher, and my mother claimed, truth is not always the most important thing in life. Like Napoleon, I discovered that where you are and who's around you can be more important.

Sometimes it's not the truth, but the timing and the audience that really matters.

Linda Ireland is a freelance writer, editor, and artist who, after many decades of wandering from Iowa to California, to Minnesota, and back to Iowa, now lives again in Waterloo, next door to the house where she grew up. The willow tree is gone, along with a number of people she once knew, but the memories live on. Linda edits books, writes, teaches drawing and painting, and enjoys scrapbooking and gardening. She has discovered that you can go home again, if you don't mind living in the Twilight Zone.

Photo provided by
Linda Ireland

Photo provided by Betty Hembd Taylor

HOMETOWN CLAIM TO FAME
Betty Hembd Taylor

I grew up near an Iowa town that was named for a site a short distance away, the Ocheyedan Mound. With a population of less than 600, Ocheyedan isn't noted for a lot, but until the early 1970s the Mound put us not only on the map, but also into reference books. At 1,675 feet above sea level, it was listed as the highest point in Iowa.

Ocheyedan, a Native American word, means "a place of mourning." The Mound was once thought to have been a burial ground, but geologists have disproved that theory. I remember it as a place for hiking and sledding parties, Fourth of July fireworks, and Easter Sunrise Services.

In the 1940s a neighbor girl, Iris Lintner, brought an unusual picture to our rural school. It showed an Easter Sunrise Service on the Mound in the 1920s. Iris's mother, who was a high school music teacher at the time, was directing the choir that morning when uninvited guests appeared. Dressed in robes and hoods, members of the Ku Klux Klan approached the worshippers from two sides, then stood quietly by as they listened to the hymns. Nervously, Faith Lintner continued to lead the music. When the singing ended, the robed visitors left as they had come, without a word.

During my high school years, it was not unusual for groups to have moonlit sledding parties on the Mound. Neither was it unusual for someone to end up with a broken bone before the season ended. One evening I attended such a party with a youth group from our church. A snow fence partially blocked our ascent, so some of us decided to climb over instead of walking around it. I tore the seat of my pants on that fence, and for the rest of the evening I brushed snow away after each descent.

That same evening my brother had a handful of friction matches in his front pocket. They were the type that would light when scratched on any surface—even on the seat of his pants. Gordon wasn't thinking of those matches when, with sled in both hands, he ran part way down the hill, belly-flopped onto it, and descended the slope at top speed. A rock hidden in the snow brought the sled to an abrupt stop, but Gordon continued to skim along on his stomach. Friction caused the matches in his pocket to ignite, and he could not extinguish them until all the sulfur was consumed, leaving a huge burn on his right thigh.

In the late fifties a local Cub Scout leader, Shirley Swenson, came up with a clever idea for the hillside. She and a group of boys gathered rocks from the surface, painted them white, and arranged them near the top to spell MOUND. The rocks stayed in place for a time, but before long someone rearranged them to spell something else. Rearranging rocks captured the imagination of many, and soon it became a tradition that has lasted more than fifty years. I seldom see anyone working on the hillside, but I almost never see the same words twice when driving by.

Shirley Swenson continued to have the Cub Scouts repaint rocks for many years. One time she and the boys climbed the hill with paint and a bucket of water to wash their hands, only to find that they were short of brushes. Not one to be deterred, Shirley instructed the boys to dip the palms of their hands into the paint and go on about the task. They had the best time that afternoon and gave new meaning to the words "hand-painted rocks."

It is an Easter tradition for members of the local Christian Reformed Church to erect three wooden crosses at the crown. On at least one occasion, I LOVE JESUS was just below the crosses, literally written in stone.

I took two grandsons to the Mound to spell out their last name when they were in second and fifth grades. Although it was a big job, they not only worked tirelessly but also ran up and down the hill from time to time to see how it looked from below.

In the summer of 2010, my extended family held a reunion in the Ocheyedan town park. After enjoying our picnic dinner, twenty-six of the hardiest souls drove to the Mound, climbed it, and spelled out our family name, HEMBD. The family name was replaced the following day, but we have pictures to prove that it really did happen.

According to the abstract filed in the Osceola County Court House, the original owner, William Mowthorpe, homesteaded the quarter section of land that includes the Mound. For several years after gaining ownership in 1888, he periodically sold some of the vast amounts of sand and gravel, leaving a scar on its crest.

Ten years later Mowthorpe sold the land to George R. Sokol, who in 1909 sold it to his daughter, Blanche, wife of W. D. Shuttleworth. Even though the supply of sand and gravel was undoubtedly worth a small fortune, the Sokols and Shuttleworths saw aesthetic and geological values in leaving the Mound as it was.

W. D. was a legendary character. Following is an excerpt from an account written by his oldest granddaughter, Margaret Vernallis:

Nannie (Blanche) *told the story of how he came to Sibley: He had an argument with his father, who had berated him for damaging a new shoe instead of expressing relief that the errant axe had spared his foot. He left, as his older brothers did before him, likely with food and coins his mother provided to him as well as his younger brother. He did as young men did in those days, likely riding the rails, hopping off to get some work, hopping back on. The Sibley lumberyard was in need of a strong young man. He was hired and so he stayed.*

One of his jobs was to deliver wood to the schoolroom of a pretty teacher. Perhaps she asked for, or he brought small enough amounts that many trips were required. In due course they were married.

Descendents of W. D. and Blanche owned the property for four generations. A great-granddaughter, Jane Shuttleworth, was influenced by generational attitudes about preserving the landscape. She became a naturalist and now coordinates Environmental Education at Iowa Lake Side Laboratory on Lake Okoboji. Jane notes that through the years family members made various attempts to donate the Mound to the State of Iowa, with the stipulation that it would be permanently preserved and maintained for the public good. Because the state had no preserves system to manage the property, early offers were declined.

The Iowa State Preserves System was organized in 1965. In 1979 they wrote to William Shuttleworth, at last expressing interest in assuming ownership of the Mound. When Jane graduated from college the following year, she came across her father's letter and learned that he had been too preoccupied to respond. William suggested that Jane could take over the project, and she managed the transfer. The gift of the Mound to the Iowa Natural Heritage Foundation was finalized on December 22, 1983. The State of Iowa turned the property and the responsibilities over to the Osceola County Conservation Board in 1985.

During the years that the Mound was privately owned, sheep grazed on its surface and kept it neatly mowed. Today the grass grows as tall as nature allows, and a trail invites hikers to make the climb. Taller grass lends too much cushion beneath the snow to make sledding, a favored winter sport of the past, work very well.

Signs at the site tell of its geological history. The Mound, of glacial origin, is a *kame*. During the Ice Age, glaciers carried sand and gravel along with larger rocks and boulders throughout the area. The glaciers deposited those materials at the mouths of ice tunnels or channels, forming kames. The Mound, which presides over the Ocheyedan River flood plain, is the largest one in Iowa.

Signs and reference material no longer define the Mound as the highest point in Iowa. Around 1971, a new survey showed that the elevation is a mere 1,655 feet and lower than land on the Sterler farm about eighteen miles away—on a hog lot near Sibley. From 1972 until 1979, the presumed location of the highest place was changed several times. One writer speculated that it moved around according to the location of the biggest hog.

In 1998, dignity returned to Iowa's highest point. The Osceola County Conservation Board removed a few structures, including a hog feed bunker, and marked the site. Governor Branstad signed a document naming Hawkeye Point, at 1,670 feet, as the highest point in Iowa. It is five feet lower than the earlier recorded height of the Mound. We can only speculate that things may have been different had the original owner not sold some of the sand and gravel from the summit.

The survey may have stripped the Mound of its claim to fame as far as elevation is concerned, but the site maintains its prestige as a geological treasure. I fondly recall the days when *World Book Encyclopedia* identified the Ocheyedan Mound as "The Highest Point in Iowa." Visitors from other states are often amused when they see it. Compared to more spectacular sites and heights they've seen, it's just a grassy hill, but to those of us with ties to Ocheyedan, it is our grassy hill, and we are proud of it.

Betty Hembd Taylor grew up listening to a litany of stories from her parents as well as an endless supply of aunts and uncles. From their collective memories, she learned to value place, time, and relationships, concepts she aspires to embody in her own writing.

Post Card provided by Betty Hembd Taylor

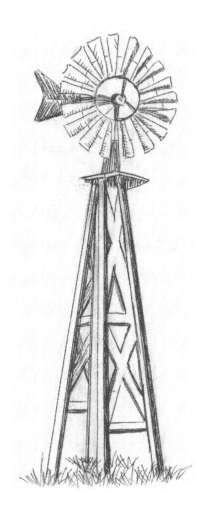

COMING IN 2012:

SOWING WILD OATS: Fifth in the Series of Stories About Growing Up in and Around Small Towns in the Midwest

If you have a true story to share about growing up in the Midwest, we'd like to see it.

For submission guidelines:
www.shapatopublishing.com/submissions

Send as an email attachment to:
Jean@shapatopublishing.com.

Or mail to:
Shapato Publishing, LLC
PO Box 476
Everly, IA 51338

Deadline: April 31, 2012

Word Count: 600 – 1600

ORDER FORM

Mail Order Form to: Shapato Publishing
PO Box 476
Everly, IA 51338

Make Hay While the Sun Shines
*Fourth in the Series of Stories About Growing Up in and
Around Small Towns in the Midwest*

Amber Waves of Grain
*Third in the Series of Stories about Growing Up in and Around
Small Towns in the Midwest*

Knee High by the Fourth of July
*More Stories of Growing Up in and Around Small Towns
in the Midwest*

**Walking Beans Wasn't Something You Did With
Your Dog**
*Stories of Growing Up in and Around Small Towns in the
Midwest*

Each $14.00
Plus sales tax each .98

S&H per quantity: 1 – 3 books $3.00

Enclosed is check or money order for: $_____
Payable to **Shapato Publishing**.

NAME: _____

ADDRESS: _____

Made in the USA
Lexington, KY
03 January 2015